The Greatest
Wild Gobblers

Lessons Learned from
Old Timers and Old Toms

Larry Dablemont

Larry Dablemont 5-22-99

Illustrations by
Tom Goldsmith

BARNABAS PUBLISHING SERVICES
Springfield, MO

Table of Contents

Tom Goldsmith

Introduction

If you've never hunted the wild gobbler in the spring, maybe you'd best put this book down. Because if you get started at it, wild turkey hunting will get in your blood and you'll sit around during the rest of the year thinking about April. If you hear an old tom gobble from the roost at the first light of day and you know he's answering that feeble little yelp you just produced with trembling hands, you won't ever be the same.

And when you first see that bright red head contrasting with the green buds before you and the wide-spread tail fan which turns your direction as a ground-raker of a gobbler eases slowly toward you... from that point on you'll be hooked. When hunting wild gobblers gets in your blood, it will be there forever.

In my years as an outdoor writer and photographer, I've had a chance to hunt and fish in a lot of places for a variety of species. I've seen the mountains in the west and wilderness lakes of Canada, the cornfields of pheasant country and the grasslands where prairie grouse and mule deer abound. Walleyes and whitetails, mallards and muskies, bass and bobwhites... I've chased them all with rod, gun and camera. But a wild gobbler in all his spring splendor, takes a back seat to nothing. If you've never been there with the redbud blossoms and the barred owls and the beginning of a new day, just a stones throw from a roosting tom which shakes the branches with his first gobble.. then maybe it's best you don't go.

It just might ruin you every April, as it has done to so many of us who hear gobblers in our sleep, and dream of the great ones we have encountered.

Maybe the title of this book is misleading, because I really can't say which of those gobblers of past hunts provided the greatest challenge. There have been lots of them and most of them stayed out there in the woods where I found them. But then again, I brought home a few of them. In my 30 years of hunting, I've killed 78 gobblers in the spring, and I'm proud to say all of them were legal.

In the pages of this book, you'll read about many of them and about some very good turkey hunters I had the opportunity to hunt with in years gone by. You may indeed find in these pages the greatest of the wild gobblers I hunted, the ones I remember best. But there's not enough room for them all because every hunting trip is a great day and every gobbler something special to recall.

When I go back over them one at a time, I think I remember the one that was the best and then I remember another one that was even better and then another one that was better yet, but in a different way than the first two. And then I begin to remember what made those turkey hunts what they came to be. Was it really a gobbler over the shoulder late in the day? That's when I get to thinking about how the woods look on an April morning when everything is still and the first rays of sun filter down through the trees to highlight a dogs-tooth violet or a wild pansy newly opened to the world and wet with dew. That's when I remember finding a cluster of morel mushrooms when the morning is late and the woods are filled with the songs of birds, or the gurgling of a small rivulet brought on by a spring thundershower which passed in the night. It comes back to me how warm the sunshine feels as the early chill is chased away and you lie on your back in a nest of thick dead leaves dozing off to the protest of bluejays in a nearby dogwood tree where blossoms are just beginning to drop their petals. It's then that I hear it, in the valleys of my memory... that distant gobble of a wild turkey tom as he sends forth his passionate announcement, I am here and ready, wild and free, wary and worthy of your best efforts. And it's then I realize that the greatest wild gobbler isn't one from days gone by, not the biggest nor the wariest nor the toughest to call, not the one with the longest beard nor the sharpest spurs. The greatest gobbler is the one that awaits each of us this coming spring and in future spring seasons to be remembered forever. No doubt about it, the greatest wild gobbler is the next one.

Chapter One

The First One
I Ever Saw

I saw my first wild gobblers in the last few days of October, 1960. They were along the Big Piney river in what was known then as the Lewis and Clark National Forest. I had no way of knowing what a tremendous effect those great wild birds were going to have on my life.

I was already 13 years old and had seen darn near everything, from baldpates and bald eagles to blue herons and blue-winged teal. I had been floating the Big Piney river with my dad since I was eight or nine but we had never encountered a wild turkey until that fall day when 10 or 12 of them flew across the river before us. They were close and they were magnificent.

We floated the river in wooden john-boats which my dad and grandfather made and we hunted almost everything from those boats — ducks, squirrels, deer, and eventually wild turkey, but not at that time of course. The Missouri Conservation Commis-

1

sion had been working for years on the restocking of wild turkeys and it was working. In only a few years there would be a regular spring season. But seeing a wild gobbler in 1960 was an event, something akin to seeing a mountain lion or a bear.

That day in October, almost 40 years ago, the turkeys didn't know we were anywhere around. We were hunting ducks and had a brush blind attached to the bow; oak and willow and sycamore limbs woven into a wire frame which allowed us to float slowly downstream completely hidden from everything below us. We had just stopped for dinner above a place known as the High-Logway eddy, so named from days of river tie-rafting decades before. There on the sand bar we saw their tracks, plain and fresh. I marveled at the size of them, and wished that just once I could see a real live wild turkey. I didn't know that I was about to see my first flock, close-up and personal. Thirty minutes after our lunch break, we floated along a couple of hundred yards below that sand bar and the air was suddenly filled with the wing-beats of large black birds. One or two or three at a time, they flew across the river only 30 or 40 yards below us alighting in the timber on the other side, seemingly unalarmed and milling about as the whole brood came across.

I got a closer look the following Saturday at

another flock. Dad had spied a flock of woodducks below a shoal, and he figured we couldn't float through the riffle without scaring them, so he pulled the boat to the bank and told me to wait. He would walk down the bank, flush the woodies back upstream and as they passed me, I would likely get a

At camp in the Ozark mountains of north Arkansas, I show off a pair of big gobblers taken on the same morning about four hours apart. In Arkansas in the mid 1980s, taking 2 gobblers In one day wasn't an uncommon feat.

good shot.

Dad had scarcely climbed over the high bank before he was in the middle of a flock of turkeys, and they flushed to fly across the river almost over the top of me. I followed several of them with my gun barrel wishing I could shoot one, but knowing better. I couldn't imagine then that in only a few years I would get my chance to hunt wild gobblers in the Ozarks.

The following spring, Missouri opened it's first legal turkey season of modern times, allowing hunters to take one gobbler. The season only lasted a few days and I remember how fascinated I was to hear one of my teachers, Coach Glenn Weaver, at Houston High School, talk about his first experiences with wild gobblers. Coach would go out for awhile each morning before school and he would come back and tell me all about it. One morning he brought his box call to school to demonstrate the fine art of calling a wild turkey. It was fascinating and I couldn't wait to learn.

That first year a local hunter, Nolan Hutcheson, killed one of the first legal gobblers in southern Missouri in many, many years. I didn't know then what a good friend Mr. Hutcheson would become as I grew older. But I saw that first gobbler and he told me all about the hunt. Nolan would, in years to come, have the distinction of being the only Missouri hunter to fill his tag each and every season, spring and fall, for a thirty or forty year period. It was a phenomenal achievement, but Nolan had a real edge on every one else. He was one of Texas county's wealthiest men, having made a considerable amount of money in the oil business and he invested it in timbered land situated on several tributaries to the Big Piney and the Jacks Fork rivers. Before the Conservation Commission even got started real good with turkey restocking in the early 1950s, Nolan began to buy and release wild turkeys on land he owned hoping those birds, which had both Rio Grande and Eastern Gobbler strains in their ancestry, would reproduce and take hold with the small fragments of wild turkey flocks he felt he already had. He did more than just buy them and turn them loose. Nolan watched over those birds, fed them through the harsh winter months and protected them from poachers. Conservation Commission biologists couldn't have done it better, or enjoyed greater success.

Nolan was much older than me, but in years to come he would become a good friend and I talked to him extensively about his experiences as a turkey hunter. Thanks to Nolan, I had a place to hunt in later years. He allowed me to hunt turkeys on land he owned, and you'll find more about him and his experiences in a latter chapter of this book. There were a number of turkey hunters back in the sixties and seventies who got a good start thanks to Nolan, a pioneer in Ozark turkey hunting.

In 1970, I graduated from the University of Missouri with a B.S. degree in wildlife management. I knew it was doubtful I could become a biologist. I had worked lots of hours to pay for my education, sometimes 30 hours or better a week. It didn't leave much time for studying. And I didn't much like studying anyway. Therefore, I didn't have the grades or the money to get into graduate school. My new wife and I moved to Arkansas in January of 1970, and I got a job as Outdoor Editor for the Arkansas Democrat newspaper in Little Rock.

Working closely with the Arkansas Game and Fish Commission, I met a gentleman by the name of Gene Rush, who was a true conservationist and an avid turkey hunter. In April of that year he invited me to hunt turkeys with him in the Ouachita mountains of Arkansas, in a G and F wildlife management area known as Muddy Creek. I don't know how it got that name. There was very little mud in the Ouachita National Forest, which covered nearly a half million acres. The streams were clear, with rock bluffs and blossoming redbuds and dogwoods everywhere. The mountains were truly mountains with deep valleys and high flat ridges, where a turkey hunter could get lost without much effort. I stood at dawn on one of those mountain tops with Gene Rush, and for the first time in my life heard wild gobblers sounding off beneath me. And on the second morning of our hunt, I passed up my first opportunity at a tom because I couldn't clearly see a beard. Rush called the bird in, but it was a jake and didn't gobble.

I didn't know it then, but I would have many more experiences with wild gobblers in the Ouachita mountains of west Arkansas, one of the most beautiful places in all the world to hunt turkeys. In fact, I would learn more about turkey hunting in those mountains in a short period of time than I would ever have dreamed possible from an old veteran hunter who knew more about wild gobblers than anyone I've ever known. His name was Clyde Trout. And if there's any part or this book you'll enjoy, it will be the chapter about that remarkable hunter who became one of my best friends. Clyde taught me most of what I know about turkey hunting, and over the years the wild gobblers in this book taught me the rest.

Chapter Two

One Foot On The Panic Button

He is a creature never more than an eye-blink away from all-out panic and there's not a thread of natural curiosity about him. If you hunt the wild gobbler, you must understand that much about him — anything out of place, any movement he doesn't expect, any sound that isn't a normal part of his surroundings will send him into headlong flight, head low and kicking up leaf litter in retreat.

Nothing I've ever hunted displays the wariness of a wild gobbler, no other species more fascinating in its natural history. And if you intend to hunt him, you need to know something more about him than how to imitate a hen.

It's his wariness that saves him. You'll hear hunters talk about how smart he is; what an intelligent creature, this wild gobbler. Well that's nonsense. His brain is small, and his intelligence of little

---

There isn't anything about the gobbler that indicates wisdom, and he has no natural curiosity whatsoever. But wary... he'll panic at the slightest indication that something is out of place.

9

significance. I've seen them do some really stupid things, like sticking their heads through a woven wire fence, trying to go through a fence they could have easily hopped over. No it's not brains. It is that propensity to run at the splat of a raindrop on a dry leaf or the distant rumble of a jet plane breaking the sound barrier. He lives with one foot on the panic button and totally without the curiosity that almost all wildlife species display to some extent.

White-tail deer survive by using a tremendous sense of smell and a very good sense of hearing. They don't see well. Many think they have no concept of color. With the wild turkey, it is their eyes that keep them alive. They hear fairly well and apparently have a very poor sense of smell. Thank goodness. One old time turkey hunter I remember once said of the wild gobbler, "If he could smell at all, you'd never get close to him, even on the upwind side."

What he doesn't have is made up for with that eyesight. The experts have deduced that they have vision comparable to what you might have with eight power binoculars. I don't know how anyone could figure that out, but it doesn't matter. They see extremely well and they discern color much better than we do, something typical of most birds. If you sit stone-still against a tree trunk, a gobbler might walk fairly close and not see you but he will pick up the slightest movement of a hunter or predator at a considerable distance.

No other species has come so close to the brink of extinction in the Midwest in recent times, with the possible exception of the woodduck. From the late '20s until the 1950s, Missouri and neighboring states had only a few scattered flocks with small numbers of birds. Everyone knows the story of their comeback, of biologists who captured birds to stock by using bait and cannon nets. It is almost inconceivable that so many birds came from such humble beginnings.

But the Eastern Wild Turkey is prolific and strong. One hen usually lays eight to fifteen eggs and will usually attempt to re-nest if the eggs are destroyed. That's one of the things that complicates hunting. Biologists plan the season so that most of the mating should be over, with hens sitting on the nests brooding eggs, when the season begins. When it works that way gobblers come to a call much better. But that response to a call isn't the natural way of things. When there is intense mating activity the hens go to the tom and the gobbling gives them the location of the gobbler on his strutting and mating area.

But there are always a few hens that aren't incubating eggs even in the peak of the nesting season and when hens come off the roost and run to a gobbler it's hard for the hunter to lure him away.

Hens and gobblers usually finish mating by 8:00 or 9:00 a.m. and the hen lays one egg per day in a simple, well hidden nest. Until the last egg is laid, she won't sit and attend the nest. Incubation begins sometimes two weeks after the first egg is laid. After about four weeks of incubation, they all hatch at the same time.

For a time, hens and poults are very vulnerable, because during nesting and for two or three weeks after hatching the hen stays on the ground at night. It takes three weeks for poults to develop flight feathers which give them the ability to gain the branches for their protection, but they don't roost in trees until they are five or six weeks old. They are threatened more by cool rainy weather during their first month of life than anything else, because until the down is well replaced by feathers, they'll die if they don't stay dry.

Some poults will hatch as late as August, probably because 50 to 60 percent of all nests are destroyed by snakes, crows, skunks, raccoons or other predators. A large number of nests are destroyed by haying machinery each year, and often the brooding hens are killed while on the nest during haying time. But those same hayfields are a dinner table in late summer and fall to young turkeys which can't get enough to eat in oak-hickory woodlands. Insects and grubs found in grassy fields will sustain them until sometime in October.

Some old-timers believed the wild gobblers would destroy nests if they found them, in order to keep the hens ready for mating over a longer period of time. I'm not sure if there's anything to that, but there will always be a limited amount of mating well into the summer and gobblers may be heard at any time during the summer months. In fact, I've heard wild toms gobble during every month of the year and

Old toms don't usually go to the hens. The hens come to them. That's what makes them so hard to call.

even in the middle of the night when startled by a sudden noise.

Once in mid-October, I watched juvenile gobblers gobbling on the roost, their beards scarcely protruding from the breast feathers. And one year while duck-hunting a small pothole just off the Osage river in western Missouri in late December, a tom began to gobble on a wooded ridge across from us. It was a warm, sunny morning and I guess he thought it was spring. I began to call to him, imitating a hen with my mouth, and he responded. In an hour he was in the open across the pothole and as I continued to call he would gobble and strut. Eventually he came all the way around that small lake, looking for the hen he thought he was hearing.

Broods shift to a greater degree of woodland activity after first frost, and feed on acorns almost exclusively during some winter periods when they are available. Turkeys love to eat greenery when spring approaches and biologists say the Vitamin A in spring green growth is one of the factors triggering gobbling as a prelude to mating. But they know too that hard winters which cause gobblers to lose sufficient body weight will have an adverse affect on spring gobbling activity.

There's little doubt that a hunter's best chance is the two-year old toms which will usually make up a great percentage of the breeding populations. Juveniles can breed and they are sometimes seen strutting and gobbling in the absense of mature dominant gobblers which have been taken by hunters. But juveniles are not the hunter's prize. They are wary, but not nearly as hard to fool, slower to spook than mature birds. They are discerned by uneven tail feathers, with central feathers longer than those to the side and usually a lighter coloration at the outer edge of the tail.

Eastern Wild Turkey are bigger now than they were 100 years ago. Back then a mature tom almost never exceeded 20 pounds in weight, some old toms would go only 17 or 18 pounds. Today toms regularly weigh from 22 to 26 pounds and there are some weighing even more. It is possible for a wild gobbler to live 10 or 12 years, but any tom reaching four or five years of age is a rare bird. Biologists discern their age by spur length which is reliable only to about the age of four.

Surprisingly, the Eastern Wild Gobbler is less of a woodland bird today. He thrives in heavy forest, or field and woodlot environments where fringes of trees are used for roosting more than anything else. They are often drawn to the fields of dairy farms where they find undigested grain in cattle manure, and now in northern states like Iowa, Minnesota and Wisconsin, they survive with pheasants around cropfields feeding on waste grain. Slender tracts of woodlands along creeks are a far cry from Ozark forests, but the wild turkey can live with that new environment — they just need a few trees to roost in.

But no matter how different he is today than his ancestors, he is no less wary. And if, on some spring morning in the Ozarks you are fortunate enough to fool a mature tom into response, you are still a long way from bagging a gobbler. If you haven't learned that from experience, you will.

Chapter Three

Turkey Hunting Tips

O ld time turkey hunter Clyde Trout used to say, "A wild gobbler always... does what he wants to. But he never knows what he wants to do until he does it." It was his way of saying that turkeys are unpredictable, and that is the only certainty to hunting turkeys. A gobbler will occasionally cross a canyon in a matter of minutes running to your call, but that doesn't happen enough. And sometimes a gobbler that has stayed just out of gun range for days will finally come to a persistent hunter.

I remember a spring hunt when one mature gobbler strutting before a hen, ignored her and then strutted 50 or 60 yards into range of my gun after only one call. But I've watched other times when toms with hens completely ignored me. That's what inexperienced turkey hunters have to come to realize — there isn't any certain pattern to the way spring gobblers behave.

That's why all those folks who win turkey calling championships sometimes can't call in a gobbler and why sometimes a beginner calls in a

gobbler on his first attempt. Calling may be a part of turkey hunting, but it's not the most important part. A wild gobblers hearing is so keen that a hunter doesn't need to call as loud as he thinks he does. Mouth calls account for a great deal of failure because few hunters call soft enough with them. When a turkey stalls 80 or 100 yards away after responding, I believe it's often because the call just isn't right, and usually too loud. Diaphragm mouth calls have surely saved a tremendous number of gobblers. This is not to say that diaphragm calls are not effective. They are great for windy conditions or mountainous country where you use a loud yelp just to get a response from a distant gobbler. But it takes a great deal of time and practice to make the mouth calls sound just right and I can't tell you the number of times I've heard somebody who thought he was really good with a mouth call that really sounded awful. Usually those people are asking me why they can get a gobbler to come up within 80 yards or so and then stop. When the gobbler gets close, the mouth calls are very often just too loud. I have never used one because I learned years ago to call with my mouth without the diaphragm device. On several occasions I have called in gobblers in such a manner,

---

You'll come to learn, in time, that there's no great magic to using a turkey call... and everyone's a beginner when they kill their first gobbler.

usually when rain or wet conditions kept me from using anything else. While small, soft calls, like slate and wood boxes have disadvantages, since they require the use of the hands, they allow inexperienced hunters to have a greater chance for success. And even after 30 years of hunting I prefer them. I'll grant you they are not the calls you want to use if you want to enter calling contests, but if you are a hunter interested in calling a wild gobbler to killing range those old reliable calls will do the best job for you. Clyde Trout use to say that he liked the old Lynch box calls so well because you could drop one and it sounded like a turkey.

The eyes of a gobbler are his greatest defense. I don't know how much better his eyes are than mine, but I can tell you with certainty, they are much, much better.

A gobbler's biggest predatorial enemy is the owl and the bobcat is next. Thirty years of hunting them has convinced me the gobbler often sees your eyes, because he's conditioned to look for the eyes of predators.

When he's close, he may see nothing more than the blink of a pair of eyes. It really is important to camouflage your face, your hands and your gun. It won't always make a difference if you don't, but sometime, somewhere, sooner or later it will cost you a wild turkey. I don't like to use the head nets because they sometimes restrict peripheral vision and get off center when you turn your head. Green, brown and black face paint is a mess to put on and take off, but it does a better job for me.

When setting up to call a gobbler, stay out of the sunlight if at all possible. Never sit in the sunlit areas... get into a dark, shaded spot and sit low. Make yourself hard to see and keep movements to a minimum. With seasons which begin in early April and end in mid-May, there is a world of difference in the woodland growth at the beginning of the season and the end. That's something hunters sometimes don't cope with very well. At the beginning of the season it is much more difficult to be well-hidden because the buds and leaves are scarce. Then at the end, there's often so much growth you can't see the gobbler until he gets fairly close. Getting hidden in a way that allows you to see well and keeps you from being seen is a real art and there are some hunters that never master it very well. I had problems when I was a beginner, thinking I could get behind a tree and look around it. That doesn't work. If the tree is between you and your gobbler he sees the movement of your head as you peer around it much better than if you sit in front of the tree and remain very still. Clyde Trout always used his knife to cut a few sprigs to place before him, just stuck down into the dirt. It didn't hide him, it just broke up the outline of his body. And I knew another hunter who carried an old umbrella with him when turkey hunting in sparsely-foliated woodlands. He had a large chunk of camouflage material where the umbrella fabric had been removed. When he worked a gobbler he sat against a big tree with that umbrella spread before him and the handle pointing back between his knees. With the "leaf-o-flage" material thrown over the ribs it looked like a bush with dead leaves. At first I laughed at him for that, but later I had to admit it worked very well because the top of the umbrella came to eye level and it was easy to aim a gun over the top of it.

When I was just starting out positioning was the hardest thing to learn. I remember a spring morning when a gobbler sounded off so close to me I had no time to pick a good spot so I sat down in a small bare spot surrounded by cedar and multiflora rose. That turkey came to within 10 or 15 yards of me and gobbled and strutted for most of an hour all around me. But I was so hidden deep in that thick cover I never did see him. I finally gave up and tried to sneak out of there, but he snuck out a great deal more effectively than I did. If you could have seen a movie of that, you would have rolled on the floor with laughter.

Not all gobblers come straight to you of course, some will circle and if they aren't gobbling as they move, they are the tough ones to get. Many years back, I was calling a wild turkey that had answered me dozens of times, finally becoming quiet about 10:00a.m. I waited and called for an hour after his last gobble, leaning up against an old oak tree with quite a bit of vegetation before me. The sun was warm and I dozed off, convinced that the gobbler had left me and was a half mile away with two or three hens. He awakened me with a gobble that shook the leaves around me, probably only 10 or 15 feet on the other side of the tree I was leaning against. The moist leaves and my state of suspended consciousness had kept me from hearing him. The last gobble brought me to wide-eyed attention, but I knew I wouldn't be able to scurry around that tree and get off a sure killing shot, so I waited. He went the other direction. There is no good instruction for such a solution. Outdoor writers and turkey hunting veterans who have an answer for everything can't tell you how to bag a gobbler which is behind the tree which you are sleeping against. And I can't exactly explain why a wild gobbler can react so much quicker than you can and make himself so hard to get a shot at before he gets out of range. But you'll find out how it is when it happens to you. You get the gobblers sometimes when you see them before they see you. When they see you first, you seldom win.

When hunters fail to see a gobbler which has answered a call and moves closer and closer it's sometimes because the turkey, 70 or 80 yards away, sticks his head up over a ledge or rock, or around a tree and sees something a little out of place. He ducks down and disappears and the hunter never knows what happened. But lack of patience causes many hunters to fail where they might have succeeded.

My biggest problem is sitting in one spot when a turkey has become quiet, even though after all these years I know he's probably still right there, very close and still interested. I like to call in gobbling, strutting toms, not one that moves in silently like a bronze ghost in forest shadows.

And always, I am sitting there I thinking that maybe if I went somewhere else I might get another tom to respond. Very good turkey hunters sit and wait, and wait and wait. Sometimes the wait is for nothing, but often a hunter who waits an hour or two after a gobbler shuts up either hears him again or sees him again.

My old friend Clyde was the best turkey hunter I ever knew for two reasons. He knew all about wild turkeys and he had the patience to sit down in a good spot at daybreak and still be there at mid-morning. But if you have problems being that patient there's another way to hunt gobblers, by walking slowly and quietly, stopping often to call and listen and hope for a response. Such a hunter needs to know the terrain well. That's a very important part of hunting wild gobblers, knowing the ridge tops and the draws, the saddles and spurs, where the creeks run and where gobblers like to roost and feed. I don't do much spring scouting, except to listen at dawn before the season. I don't like to get out and mingle with gobblers before the season and I don't call them in an area I'm going to hunt. But if you are going to hunt a new area it's a good idea to walk through it and explore it well before the season, preferably in February or early March.

Beginners, and inexperienced hunters make the same mistakes. They sometimes hide so well they can't see the gobbler, or they hide so poorly he sees them. They try to move a gun barrel slowly as a gobbler moves in and he spooks at the movement. They get too excited and try to kill a gobbler out of range, one that may have been in their lap had they waited. They call too much or too little. Usually it's the latter, because novice hunters never believe they can make a call sound right. They don't stay put long enough and they leave the woods too early in the morning to go to the local coffee shop and complain about the hunting.

And inexperienced hunters very often have trouble estimating the distance of a gobbler they hear. There are many factors which cause this to happen; wind, the lay of the land, the direction the gobbler is facing and the stage of spring greenery which absorbs sound. You learn to figure that distance only with experience — that's the only way. But even when a novice hunter does pinpoint a gobbler, he very often tries to move too close. If you can get to within 60 yards or so, it's a great deal easier of course, but it doesn't often work unless the wind is strong, or you have a big rock wall between you and the gobbler. Remember he can see you and hear you so much easier than you think be can. As a rule, you'll get more gobblers calling them from 150 yards away than trying to sneak in close. Oh sure, I know, I didn't believe it either. Again, experience and several wary old gobblers will teach you.

The funny thing is, even veteran turkey hunters continue to learn with experience. We all make the same mistakes, year after year, and discover new mistakes which can be made. That's why every year in June, there are a number of wild gobblers still walking around with long beards and sharp spurs. In closing, I'll stress that hunters who fail are hunters who try to sneak up on turkeys, call too loud, can't sit still and come in before 10 a.m. for breakfast.

That's why, every spring so many turkey hunting stories begin with, "I should've..." or "If only..." And they end with "Next time..."

Chapter Four

The Turkey Scout

*P*re-season scouting isn't easy, it involves getting up before daylight and sometimes making your own breakfast. I have a difficult time doing either one. It gets easier though at first light. To properly scout for turkeys you must listen for gobblers at daylight, usually from a pickup with windows rolled down, where some gravel road travels high ground.

Everyone has a different method of scouting. Some hunters leave the pickup and walk 40 or 50 feet away. Others sit on a tailgate or a fender and drink coffee while listening.

Every year about a month or so before turkey season some of the urban outdoor writers come out with their advice on scouting for gobblers. It conjures up images of someone in buckskin sifting through the

---

I like to scout new territory on opening day of the season, with a shotgun and a turkey call. This one came from a place I had never been before...back in 1991.

leaves for sign.

As enjoyable as it is to hear three or four old gobblers sound off on the roost at dawn, that's about as close as I care to get until opening morning unless I have a camera with me. The only thing a hunter really needs to know beyond that is the lay of the land, where the old trails and logging roads run and how the creeks and draws sit beneath the ridges. If you don't know that by April, you've probably waited too long to learn. I wouldn't be exploring too much in country I want to hunt, I'd wait until opening morning and do my scouting with a shotgun and a turkey call.

It is a definite advantage to hunt land you really know well, but it's also fun to hunt new areas. Beginning turkey hunters might study a topographical map of an area they plan to hunt if they don't know it well. If I'm in a new area I find the high ground and start there at dawn and move toward the gobblers I hear. Sometimes, you're at a real disadvantage by not knowing an area, but brother, what a challenge.

It doesn't hurt to walk the trails and old roads in an area you want to hunt, looking for scratching and droppings and that type of thing. But don't overdo it. Get the lay of the land well before the season and then stay out of it.

Now I'm not saying that a hunter walking through the woods is likely to tip off a flock of turkeys that the hunting season is nigh and send them all scurrying to heavy cover. But you can have an impact on the habits of turkeys which are beginning to go into the mating season and when a not-so-confident hunter starts practicing his call or hooting like an owl every hundred yards, it isn't likely to increase his chances over the next few weeks. I'm convinced too, that every time a gobbler responds to a call and is spooked by something he'll be just a little more difficult to call up during the same spring season. No, it's not that he's wiser because turkeys don't have any wisdom, but warier, because they have enough wariness for all the creatures in the Ozarks. When I sit down on opening morning, hopefully within a couple of hundred yards of a gobbler, I hope my call is the first one he has heard since last spring. I've noticed when I go to an area and take pictures before the season that if I call in a nice gobbler rather easily, it seldom happens with that same turkey again. If he spooks while I'm taking pictures, he'll be tough to call in the next few days.

If you intend to play with your call before the season, you should get well hidden and never let the gobbler know you are something other than a wandering hen. Shut up when he gets close, and let him stroll past into the forest thinking he has no luck at all at finding prospective hens.

To be really ready for the hunting season, pattern your shotgun and know it's limits. Beginning turkey hunters hurt themselves quite often by not having the slightest idea of the range of a turkey in the woods. They look bigger and closer than they really are and I've seen hunters shoot at gobblers 60 yards away thinking they were only 30 or 40 yards from the end of the gun barrel. You should never hunt with low powered shells and never use shot sizes smaller than sixes or larger than fours. I prefer a 3-inch magnum 12 gauge and wouldn't hunt turkeys with anything smaller. I can hear the protests of those twenty gauge hunters, or those who swear by smaller shot and two and three-quarter inch shells. If you want to be an effective and conscientious hunter, ignore them. Wild gobblers are big, strong birds and you'll lose one on occasion if you hunt with lesser fire power, or try to stretch the range of what you have.

Ten gauges, or three and one-half inch twelve gauges are guns made for geese and turkeys and they are superior in killing power at ranges up to 45 yards. Trouble is, too many hunters carry those big guns thinking they will bag a gobbler at 60 or 70 yards, and they just aren't made for that kind of distance. And I've noticed that carrying a 10 gauge, which is a considerable amount heavier, seems less and less wise as you grow older. Ten gauge owners should always hunt downhill.

You should check out your shotgun and be sure that if it's an automatic it will smoothly eject three shells, just in case you should have to fire that many shells. Not that I've ever had to... Well, at least not lately.

I also want to be sure my boots are well oiled and waxed, since wet feet are a miserable problem in the spring. And you might want to do some walking to get in shape. I walk to the mailbox every day just to get ready, and if that doesn't work, I get in shape after the season starts rather than in preparation for it.

If you are a hunter new to the sport of turkey hunting, be sure you know all about the regulations of the state where you will be hunting because from state to state there are different laws to go by. And it will help you if you are a beginner, or someone who has not had much success in past seasons, to find a farm where there are tame turkey hens to listen to. Go there and listen a lot and practice on some old tame toms while you're at it. Some people might laugh at that advice, but it is very important to know exactly how a hen turkey sounds. When I first started hunting I spent hours at Ozark farms listening to domestic hens — which call exactly like the wild ones.

I used to practice incessantly with my turkey

call when I was a beginner, but I don't do it much since my wife and daughters threatened to leave. Besides that, if you see somebody practicing with a turkey call, it's a dead giveaway that he's a greenhorn. There are other things to tip you off, of course, that a hunter is a beginner. Brand new camouflaged clothes will tell you. Experienced hunters have clothes which are ripped in the crotch from crossing barbed wire fences, worn thin in the seat from sitting on rocky timbered hillsides and faded from too many washings.

You can tell a greenhorn in the woods if you happen across one while doing your pre-season scouting. He'll talk too much. He'll tell you how many gobblers he's heard and be quite proud of it. No veteran tells anyone about hearing a gobbler. Veteran hunters, if caught scouting for gobblers, will look as if they are on the brink of quitting. They've heard nothing for days, and they'll tell you that biologists have been trapping toms in that area all winter. Some will even give you figures like: "My brother-in-law heard somebody who works for the conservation people say that they took 380 turkeys out of here in January."

A veteran will tell you about a real good spot to hunt about 15 or 20 miles away and draw you a map to help you get there. I once knew an old veteran hunter like that. He didn't do much "scouting" either, but a week or so before the season, he would walk through his favorite area and rub out every turkey track he came across. Any "scouter" who walked a logging road where that old-timer hunted would see no tracks, no droppings, no sign that a turkey had ever passed there.

I learned a lot from that old guy about evidence removal. And in my younger days, I got into crowd control. I'd take several pairs of old boots and wear each pair up and down the first 30 or 40 yards of the logging roads going into my favorite hunting area. Of course it didn't work unless there was plenty of mud, but if there was, I could make it look like there were several hunters "scouting" the area and discourage any intruders from even considering such a spot. I never had to go very far down the road to make it look crowded, but it was hard work. It's hard to walk in those size 11 and 12 boots without tripping.

Most of my getting ready for turkey season was done at home. I'd start sometime in early March sitting on my foot until it got numb. If you can sit on your foot until it no longer has any feeling you are ready to hunt turkeys. You'll do that a lot in the woods when there's a gobbler sounding off about 70 or 80 yards away and he stays there for hours. I'd also

35

practice lying flat on my belly in the leaves, rocks and gravel, aiming my shotgun with my neck at a 90 degree angle to the ground. And I'd practice hiding. I'd sit behind a potted plant in the corner of the living room in my camouflaged clothing with the lights turned down watching TV while my wife looked for me, wanting the garden tilled or some such nonsense. And that's another thing you need to remember, only beginners work on the lawn before the turkey season is over.

But in closing, let me say that you shouldn't feel bad about being a beginning turkey hunter if you are one. We all were beginners once and it's a good thing to be, because it's so much fun to learn all the things that wise old veterans know. And if you just can't contain yourself, go out before the season and listen to gobblers and walk in the woods and see if you can figure out where the most turkeys are concentrated. But please, don't call it "scouting." Call it exploring, call it getting ready, call it practicing, but just don't call it "scouting." Kit Carson would thank you if he were still with us.

Chapter Five

I Hunted Turkeys
With Clyde

I moved to the north Arkansas community of Harrison in 1973 working as a Naturalist for the National Park Service at Buffalo River. I had begun to hunt wild turkeys a couple of years before and had one or two to my credit by then. I was writing a weekly column for the Arkansas Gazette in Little Rock and had been for some time. And I had been getting letters about turkey hunting from an old gentleman from Harrison by the name of Clyde Trout. He was in his 60s and I was in my early 20s, but Clyde and I became friends in a hurry. He was the county clerk there in Harrison and a more admired and respected man you will never find.

Once I got to know him, I spent hours at his place several miles north of town talking turkey hunting. He had a little retreat built just outside his home, a place he called the "roost." There were pictures of turkeys and old turkey hunters all over the walls, gobbler beards hanging everywhere and every turkey call Clyde ever found that was a little different. We would

watch movies of turkeys he had taken with his old movie camera, because when Clyde couldn't hunt turkeys he would spend his time filming them.

In the spring of 1974, Clyde and I and another friend journeyed south to the Ouachita mountains in west Arkansas, pitched a tent and hunted wild turkeys. We would return every spring thereafter for six or eight years. Back then there weren't many hunters and plenty of gobblers. We usually always managed to get a gobbler or two and, of course, there were always one or two close calls where the gobbler came out on top.

I don't know how I could have learned more in such a short period of time. Clyde Trout knew turkeys and turkey hunting like no man I have met before or since. In the evenings, when a chill settled over the mountain valleys and the fire burned bright, I'd turn on my tape recorder and we youngsters, or "would-be'ers" as Clyde referred to us, would settle back to listen and ask questions.

There were stories enough to last for years. He told us about the first gobbler he had heard, the first one he had taken and the first one he had let get away. There was the story about the trip 30 years be-

Clyde Trout hunted turkeys year-round with his movie camera and enjoyed chasing turkeys through every season. He knew more about wild turkeys and how to hunt them, than any man I've ever met.

fore when they had to abandon an old car in the woods and walk home, the story about the time he got lost in an east Arkansas swamp and the time they had tied up a white goose for an Arkansas legislator who was on his first hunt and thought he was going to find a tied-up turkey he could shoot to take back and show his fellow hunters.

He talked about hunting Eastern Gobblers in Mississippi, and Rio Grandes in Oklahoma and about the days when hearing just one gobbler was about the most exciting thing that could happen to a hunter. Then he'd stand up and stretch and get rid of his tobacco and announce that it was time to "fly up for the night."

I remember too, how awful it was when that alarm clock went off at 4:00 in the morning and we were faced with crawling out of a warm sleeping bag to find frost all around us. When we'd finally get a fire going and some coffee on, Clyde would sit up and clear his throat and say something like, "Ain't life grand?" It always sounded like he meant, What the heck am I doing here?

But he'd usually beat us out of camp and be the last one back for dinner. And then there would be another story. I kept all those tapes we made and I thought maybe it would be best to let you hear what Clyde had to say about turkey hunting. So here it is, in his own words:

I would like to point out in the beginning that I have nothing to sell, nothing to promote or advertise, no reputation to protect, no title to defend. I don't consider myself any authority on the wild turkey. Actually, I probably don't qualify as a better-than-average turkey hunter if you consider how few feathers I've gathered per hours spent hunting.

People often ask me why I spend so much time hunting wild turkey. If you've hunted them, I don't have to tell you. If you haven't, I'd never answer the questions to anyone's satisfaction.

Certainly the activity of a gobbler hunter qualifies him as a questionable character. He will spend money he doesn't have driving mile after mile after mile. He will camp out in the wild yonder under the most adverse of conditions and will partake of food that if served at home he would withhold from his least-loved hound. He may roll out of bed after little or no sleep and take off for the timber as the very first streak of gray appears in the east.

The only tangible thing he will ever be able to show for this manifestation of vigor is possibly one blue-headed, smutty-colored bird called a wild gobbler. And sadly I must add, very often nothing. This might not seem so strange, but this same oddball will be seen repeating this operation year after year. I can't really tell you why I like to hunt wild turkey. No gobbler hunter asks why — he knows.

I was advised a long time ago by an economist that he could work for five cents per hour for the time I put in turkey hunting and buy a lot more meat than I would bring in and have money left. This happened to be a relative of my wife. Through a mixture of fear and respect for her family, I was able to suppress the answer that came to my mind fairly easily. This sagacious law-giver has long since passed on to his reward, whatever it may have been. He left behind a very modest estate, but not a single turkey beard bedecked the halls of his abode.

I have found no better way to dismiss the problems of life, than by hunting the wild turkey. I honestly could not tell you how much I owe or when the interest is due during turkey season.

When I started chasing gobblers we would drive an old car of some sort as far as the roads of that day would permit. From there we would backpack our bedding, food and guns, back into the woods from one to three miles. There we would defy the elements and set up camp with the heavens as a roof and Mother Earth as a mattress. I think with a little age we become wiser as well as losing some nerve. I would be a little cool to the idea of having to repeat the same today. However, that was the best we could do and the only chance for gobbler hunting.

As I think back, those gobblers were not in as much danger as I thought at that time. What we didn't know about gobbler hunting would fill a sizeable library. The possibilities of today compared to then is staggering. Today it's not only possible, but likely for a hunter to finish a day's work at one place and with proper connections, be back at camp with a gobbler before sunup the following morning — hundreds of miles away. And all that with probably less time involved and less physical effort then we encountered to get a scant six or eight miles from home.

The improvement in firearms, the increase of hunters, the modern means of travel and the building of roads simply tell us they have moved in on Mr. Wild Tom. The fact that he has the same equipment for rebuttal that he ever had certainly lessens the odds for his survival. His range is still the same — he can't run any faster or fly any farther. His habits are exactly the same. There's a lot less area for him to hide in. Yet he still survives to defy the best. This is living testimony that he is no pushover.

One thing of particular interest to me is that every day spent in the turkey woods is a complete story within itself. The events of the day whatever they are, are not prearranged. The outcome is not known until it's over. You control but very little of the day's actions. I like the variations that may be expected.

When I hear a gobbler and make an effort to call it, I usually expect to have it bagged and by the neck in almost less time than it takes to tell it. But in fact, I may still be pursuing it the last day of the season, or I may never hear it again. In between these extremes is a category of things that may or may not happen, that you could talk a lifetime about and never cover them all.

There are certain basic rules that you normally go by to gobbler hunt. Any gobbler hunter will tell you this. Under each rule there are sub-rules of do's and don'ts that would fill a book — with these to be used as the occasion demands. For instance, one rule is to be still. That, of course, doesn't mean you go to the turkey woods and sit down and don't bat an eye all day, but while you might win some ball games by breaking a basic rule, you'll win more by abiding by them. The same goes for gobbler hunting

I suppose the reason we take a gun along is that we want to kill a gobbler, but as I look back through the years, some of the hunts that seem to stand out more are some of the ones where the gobbler won. I actually hunt with mixed emotions. I enjoy every moment I spend in the turkey woods. If I should kill one real early the first day, it in a way, *ruins the season. I know, for I've done that. When you're allowed one gobbler, though, you may be extremely lucky to get it, early success means the fun's all over and the gobbler is dead. I suppose the ultimate would be to hunt all season and kill an old grandpa the last day. I've been blessed with this experience a few times, but not often enough.*

I have some regrets at killing one at all. You look at a wild gobbler as he stands out there like a statue, that glistening shade of varying colors, a wary monarch unequalled. Then watch as he struts, a formation the likes of which you can't describe. You lower the boom on him, then look him over after he quits flopping. You're proud of him, sure, I always am too. But he's a different bird now. Dead as a hammer. No more fun in him. Bloody head and neck, feathers all tousled and broken... doesn't even look the same. I don't really feel too bad when he gets away. It feels good when it quits hurting.

I like hunting by the rules of the game. I've tried a little both ways and like the legal way better. You may not love some of the individuals who help set or enforce our laws. You may not like all the rules. Neither do I. Overall they do a good job and need your help and mine. I would hate to think about where we would be without regulations. Those illegal turkey beards you may hang up are a little tainted, they may eventually turn a yellowish color. On the last day of a season I think at times I would be tempted to bring in a gobbler I had found dead if it wasn't too far gone. Yet I can in all sincerity tell you I wouldn't give a lead pencil to kill a gobbler with a 15-inch beard either before or after the season.

You learn the art of turkey hunting mostly by experience. I hunt all day long where the law per-

Clyde Trout and his son Larry, hunting in the north Arkansas turkey woods a few miles from his home.

mits. Whatever events may be for the rest or the day, they're denied the hunter who has long since gone home. I have heard gobblers every hour of the day from before daylight until after dark, even in the middle of the night. Many of the richer experiences I've enjoyed have happened in the still of the day that all others have dismissed for the duration.

Every gobbler hunter I know has a great deal or pride about his ability to call turkeys. Most of them think or at least wants the other fellow to think they are the best. Being able to make a sound like a turkey is an important part of the game, but not any great feat.

Over at Yellville they have an annual event known as the National Wild Turkey Calling contest. I hunt every year with a man who has won this event several different years. Of course, it would be possible to win an event of this sort and never have killed a wild gobbler. In fact, it happened. This is not the case with my friend, who is a good gobbler hunter. In order to win you have to be able to imitate very well the call of a turkey, and he can. This same hunter, I've observed, has problems like mine, sometimes he doesn't. Your ability to call won't cure all your troubles.

In almost every area I've hunted there seems to be the story of that old smart gobbler that you can't call. One that stands out above all others, until he has become a legend. This theory, whether real or imaginary, seems to be shared with a few hunters here and there. You may be one who shares this view, but I don't buy the idea. It's sure that I have never had a great deal of trouble keeping gobblers beat off me after I attempt to call one. I believe that age and experience wise up the gobbler as well as the man.

But nature has bestowed upon the turkey a means of communication and the desire to get together. No amount of age or experience nor any amount of unfriendly association with man will ever purge him of qualities given to him by nature. He may get tougher and you may fail time and again. Perseverance and technique will finally fell him if you wish to persist.

In closing, if you are a young man and need something to break the monotony, I suggest a spring gobbler hunt. I believe it will be worth your effort. I've never heard of a man who hunted gobblers committing suicide just before turkey season. I sometimes feel like it at the end, but never just before it opens.

If you should ever try it and hear a wild gobbler and you call him up to where you see him, he shows up then disappears, then shows again as he edges closer, then stops... if you can go through an ordeal like this, whether you get him or not, all the while thinking about your troubles, staying calm or truthfully saying there's nothing to it, here's my advice to you. You not only need a guardian, you need the best professional help our modern world has to offer.

A wild gobbler puts all men on the same level. I know of no other area of my life where I could be considered equal to anyone. You might be permitted to hunt where I would be barred, a lot of people are. You might have a better gun, nearly everyone does. You might be a better hunter, most of them are that also. But you set me down in the turkey woods with a king and I'm his equal. Outside of the above mentioned advantages, there's no string he can pull or no power under the shining heavens that will influence that gobbler. He's not swayed by power, money or influence and respects no one. I sort of like that thought.

I do not know that I'll ever be permitted to gobbler hunt again, but I'm planning on it now. He who holds the future in His hand has the answer. In case I do not, life in the gobbler woods owes me nothing. I have reaped more than my share-maybe not in beards hung up, but in pleasant moments spent, and pleasant memories to live with.

Before Clyde passed away, he hunted in southern Missouri with some old friends and killed his 81st gobbler. They told me that he couldn't get it back to his vehicle, someone went out and brought it back for him. Two months later Clyde was sitting in his front yard talking about wild turkeys with another old friend, when he collapsed and died of a stroke. He had expressed a fear of seeing a day when he was physically unable to hunt anymore. Perhaps that would have been a worse tragedy than the painless death which struck quickly that summer afternoon. I'll always think God looked down on him that day and said, "Clyde, you've got a lot of old friends waiting to see you and I have some beautiful woodlands filled with magnificent flocks for you to enjoy."

All of us who knew and hunted with Clyde Trout were better off for the time spent with him. And today, when some great turkey hunter is expounding on his exploits, and boasting of his accomplishments in the turkey woods, I listen politely. And if when he gets through he should turn to me and say, "What do you consider your greatest accomplishment as a wild turkey hunter?" I don't hesitate in my answer. I throw out my chest and reply with pride, "Mister, in my younger days, I hunted turkeys with Clyde Trout."

Chapter Six

"I Owed You One"

*S*ometime each spring, during the second week of April, some friends and I will travel south to the beautiful Ouachita mountains of west Arkansas, in the valley of the Fourche river, to camp and hunt where I so often hunted wild turkeys with Clyde Trout back in the 1970s. Clyde was in his late sixties, and I in my early twenties. He was an accomplished turkey hunter, maybe the best I ever hunted with... I was a beginner trying to learn all I could as quickly as possible. We went there for four or five years and as I learned and began having success, Clyde grew older and it became more difficult for him to walk up into those rugged mountains. I set up camp, brought all the gear and food and tried to make it as comfortable for him as possible. He had a favorite spot up behind our campsite where the creek forked, one branch upstream to the east, one upstream toward the south. Between them a timbered point rose gently to a long, wide ridge, and Clyde would climb that point, walk-

ing an old logging road that wound back and forth. He'd be there from dawn 'til mid-day and then again until dusk. Usually he'd have a gobbler before we had been there two or three days.

I remember the last one because I was in camp making dinner when I heard him shoot and I headed up that way to help him carry in his turkey. Halfway down the point I found him rolling the tom down the hill with his foot because it was just too heavy to carry. It was his 78th gobbler.

Clyde never returned for another hunt. Two years later he was sitting in his lawn during the summer talking about turkey hunting with an old friend when he collapsed and died of a stroke. That summer after his funeral I agreed to do some writing for a new magazine. The magazine was called "Gun Dog" and it had to do with upland bird and waterfowl hunting and the pointers and retrievers hunters used to pursue their sport. Dave Meisner, the publisher and owner of the magazine was about my age and we became friends hunting game birds and ducks that fall. He had never hunted wild turkey and was anxious to see the Ouachita mountains of Arkansas in the spring when the wild turkeys were gobblin', maybe even see

In a Ouachita mountain camp, Dave Meisner relaxes beside the gobbler which circled him and came to me.

In the majestic mountains of Arkansas' Ozark and Ouachita national forestland there were places you could hunt gobblers all alone for a whole season... if you didn't mind walking and climbing and risking getting lost.

if he could learn to hunt them.

So we camped the following April in the same old familiar campsite and though my hunting companions that year couldn't know it I could still see and hear my old friend sitting around the campfire speculating on the coming of a new spring dawn. I had no doubt that his spirit was still there with us.

It was chilly that morning when we all rose before daylight to get ready, drink coffee and eat a little breakfast. Dave Meisner was pretty excited about the upcoming hunt... especially when I told him we were going to climb up to Clyde's favorite point — a place I had never hunted.

As I remember, we heard toms on both sides of us as we selected a spot along the old logging road two thirds of the way to the top. I put Dave against a big white oak where he could see well in all directions and then I got hidden about 30 yards behind him. As the mist rose and the sky brightened in the east, one gobbler down to our left, up the south fork of the creek, was obviously interested in my call. He flew down to strut and gobble and then slowly began to move up toward the ridge-top where we waited and called.

It was one of those mornings when the woods were still, birds were singing and you were just thrilled to be there in the midst of God's greatest creation. I could see why Clyde always headed for that spot where oaks were as big around as wagon-wheels and the pines reached high and straight. And before the first sun's rays could reach the woodland floor we had a majestic gobbler climbing that point to find the location of the hen I was struggling to imitate. I remember telling myself that Meisner was certainly a lucky beginner.

Dave got a good case of buck fever when he saw that big black tom easing up the slope toward him. He got his gun in position and did everything right as the gobbler drew to about 60 yards and stopped. He stood there for quite some time and I know he wasn't spooked, or he would have been gone. But for some reason, as I continued to call, he moved in a slow circle around to our right, always out of range, but no doubt intent upon finding that hen.

He never did find her. When he had passed Dave's waiting gun, always just a little out of range and still circling, he walked straight toward me, slowly and steadily. I waited until he was in range and had his head behind a big oak tree. Then I quickly brought up the gun barrel and waited until that bright red head was high. As the gunshot echoed across the valley and the gobbler flopped wildly in his death throes, I sat back and took a few deep breaths. Somehow it seemed right then that Clyde was beside me, grinning his approval. And I could hear him saying, "I owed you that one young feller, thanks for all those years."

I always thought I was the one that owed Clyde the thanks. He taught me a great deal more than just how to hunt turkeys. It was my responsibility to pass on what I had learned and I have tried to do that. Dave killed his first gobbler in May of that year in his home state of Iowa and several more over the years. Someday I'm sure I'll camp at the old campsite again and climb the same point once more with a beginning hunter hoping to get his first gobbler. And he'll get one eventually and go on to become an expert like all the rest of us who let gobbler-hunting get in the blood. I think Clyde expected it to be that way.

Chapter Seven

Turkey Farrel

My dad, Farrel Dablemont, who still lives over in the Big Piney country where I was raised, taught me a lot of things about the outdoors. He taught me how to hunt squirrels and ducks and quail and rabbits and how to fish for bass and catfish and paddle a john-boat. But he didn't know a thing about turkey hunting, because there were none in our part of the Ozarks when he was young.

But he'll tell you today that I was the one who made him a turkey hunter. He has said many times that raising me taught him a great deal about patience. And I called up his first wild turkey.

It came about because I was living down in Arkansas and driving up to Missouri in the spring to hunt turkeys. I brought along my old friend Clyde Trout one week-end in April and we found a good tract of public land on the Piney where there were

---

In the early 1970s, my dad killed his first gobbler and became an expert overnight, just like all the rest of us. Back in those days, southern Missouri was a turkey hunter's paradise.

quite a few turkeys. I was just learning to call and couldn't afford to buy a non-resident tag at the time, so dad bought himself a tag and volunteered to shoot a gobbler if I could call one up. He and I and Clyde drove out that spring morning in my pick-up and immediately Clyde headed for a spot quite some distance from where dad and I intended to hunt.

Of course I didn't really think I could call up a gobbler, and dad didn't either. But we walked well into the woodlands and I cranked away on that old wooden box and a gobbler answered in a small hollow before us. That was a pretty exciting thing. Dad was expecting to see or hear very little and just like that, we had one interested.

He situated himself against a big tree looking down into the shallow valley and knowing it was harder to hide two hunters than one, I stepped back about 30 yards behind him, well hidden and unable to see down the hill at all. I figured I didn't need to see the gobbler. After all, dad had the gun, I didn't.

And so, the drama began. Little did we know it would turn into a comedy. My dad really didn't figure I could call up a wild turkey and I was even more skeptical than he was. But I sat back there with my box call, cranking away, and the doggone gobbler, which must have originally been a half mile away, started coming to us and continued to gobble.

Now during the week before I had been hunting with Clyde down in Arkansas trying to learn how to call gobblers. One of the things he had showed me about his box call was how well he could use it to imitate a gobbler, as well as a hen. He would rattle that thing on occasion and it would sound so real that other gobblers would answer it. I got to thinking about that while I was sitting there waiting for that ghost gobbler to materialize. It seemed he was staying in one place an awfully long time. I began to convince myself that my old friend was playing a trick on me. He was out there rattling that box call, sounding like a tom, pulling a fast one on my dad and me.

As usual, I was getting antsy. Dad and I had been there for nearly an hour and I just knew if that was a real turkey out there, he would have been in range by now. No sir, it was old Clyde. I was sure of it. And so, unable to sit there any longer, I stood up and called out to my dad, "That's not a gobbler, it's Clyde down there having some fun with us."

My dad, sitting where he could see below us, was of course watching something I could not see... a strutting wild turkey tom, inching his way up the hillside before him slowly but surely, and almost, but not quite in gun range. When I stood up and proclaimed it all to be a hoax, the gobbler left in short order. A lot of what happened after that is vague in my memory. Dad said a lot of things about my mom's side of the family and how much I was like them. He kicked a stump and limped around there for awhile with that old 97 Winchester in his hand and I have to admit I didn't feel real safe there for a short time. But then I remembered that several times when I was a kid, Dad had threatened to kill me over more serious things and he hadn't ever done it. And if you stop and think about it, he really should have signaled to me that he was watching a gobbler. Mom always said Dad was bad to blame everyone else and accept none of the responsibility.

But there were worse times ahead for dad. Clyde and I went back to Arkansas and I left the box call for him to use. He took off from work one morning and went after that gobbler again, after a considerable amount of practice with the call, and I'll be darned if he didn't call in another gobbler. As luck would have it, the bird came in on his right side, and dad, who was well hidden, couldn't get his gun around to that side. We always hunted ducks on the Big Piney by floating down the river in our john-boat, jump shooting over a blind on the bow of the boat. With ducks, dad's old long-barreled 97 Winchester pump was the last word. He was quick with it and didn't often miss. Watching that gobbler move to within about 35 yards, dad figured he had himself a turkey. All he had to do was stand up, turn to the right a little and flush the old tom, then bust him in flight. It should be a much easier and slower target than a mallard drake. That's the day dad learned about gobblers — they are quicker than lightning. They don't often fly when they can run and when they are spooked they keep their heads to the ground and their heels in the air. He stood there in a state of bewilderment wondering where the gobbler had gone.

The good news is dad finally did get a gobbler that spring, learning from his mistakes I suppose. And right away quick, he becomes an expert on turkey hunting, just like Clyde said would happen. When he called up and killed another one the next spring, he started giving advice to everyone and wanted the guys down at the pool hall to begin to call him Turkey Farrel. They wouldn't, of course. Most of his friends began to avoid him until April was over because when they saw him coming they knew they were about to get a lesson on turkey hunting.

Dad is still hunting wild turkeys with about 40 gobblers to his credit, which is not a bad total for someone who seldom hunts more than 10 miles from his house. And he has lots of stories, but one experience in particular befuddles him to this very day. It happened about twenty years ago when he was hunting some private land along the Big Piney river and spent most of the morning chasing two gobblers which were strutting and gobbling and fighting while they were ignoring him. But dad stuck with it, moving from this vantage point to another, calling here and sneaking there, setting up in one place and circling around to another until finally, several hours after he started the two gobblers decided to come to his call. He picked out the biggest one and clobbered it with a load of number 4 magnums and watched the other one run off aways and stop. So he walked up to his gobbler, which was flopping around all over the place and laid down his old shotgun while he fished around in his billfold for his tag.

As he did that, the second gobbler came charging out of nowhere and jumped on the dying tom, spurring and flogging it unmercifully. Dad wondered if he were hallucinating. He was standing less than 10 feet away and a wild gobbler was ignoring him, wreaking havoc with his trophy, kicking out big wads of feathers and wild-eyed with madness. In fact dad said just for a moment, he wondered if turkeys ever got rabies. But finally, he hauled off and kicked the turkey about six or eight feet, and reached down to pull his dying gobbler out of harms way. When he did, the downed bird, still kicking, spurred his hand and inflicted a gash which would eventually take several stitches to close. And on top of that, here came that second bird back to jump on the first one again. By now, dad was mad. When he attempted to kick the turkey away again, the gobbler began to flog his leg and try to spur him. It was more than dad could stand. He retrieved his shotgun, and kicked the crazed gobbler one last time, this time a considerable distance. The bird gathered itself, got to it's feet and headed back to renew the fight. He didn't make it. The roar or the Winchester pump gun echoed across the valley and the ordeal was over.

Dazed and bleeding, dad tagged the first tom and headed for his pick-up with his turkey over his shoulder. He left the other one there, maybe the only gobbler to ever die of absolute stupidity. Dad felt bad about it, he hadn't ever violated the one-bird-per-season rule until that day and he knew no one would ever accept his plea of self-defense.

To help him out, a friend of ours retrieved the second gobbler and tagged and checked it, so eventually dad didn't feel so bad. And what is even more remarkable the first gobbler, which had spurred him wickedly across the palm of the hand, had only one long sharp spur. The one on the other leg was gone. If dad had reached for that leg he would have escaped injury.

I know what some of you folks are thinking, but you can forget it. Dad's among the most truthful men I know. As honest as I am, he's even more honest than me and a deacon in his church as well. No, it happened just the way he said it did, I'm confident of that. But he won't talk about it much today. Dad says some things are best forgotten. If you should see a flying saucer, or a ghost, or talk to an angel, or have hand to hand combat with a wild gobbler after you have just shot his runnin' buddy it's best to just keep quiet about it. None of your friends are quite that good a friend. There will be some grinnin' and snickerin' and some folks will talk for awhile. When you get into turkey hunting, I guess that's to be expected!

Chapter Eight

The Seven Bearded Gobbler

*T*he campfire was burning low, the spring night growing cooler. At the frosty dawn of a new day in the Ouachita mountains of western Arkansas, turkey season would begin. My old friend Clyde Trout stood and gazed into the dark woodlands behind our camp before turning in for the night.

"Well, suh," he said without turning around, "somewheah out theah, a big ol gobbluh is a wrappin' his toes aroun' a limb for the las' time."

That, my friend, is confidence. Clyde never went out into the woods without the feeling that he'd have a big old ground-raker by the neck in a matter of a few hours. He was about 70 years old then, with 77 legal gobblers to his credit.

Clyde had no interest in waterfowl nor upland birds nor whitetailed deer. When the hunting season for wild turkey was closed in the summer and winter months he chased them with an old movie camera and declared that the Creator had put nothing else on

earth to equal the wild gobbler as a challenge for the hunter.

Most of the gobblers he killed were taken in the Ozark mountains of north Arkansas, or the Ouachitas in west central Arkansas, and most of them in a time when a wild turkey track attracted a crowd, there were so few of them. But he had also hunted in Mississippi and Oklahoma and Missouri, and had spent more hours hunting turkeys than any man I've ever known before or since. When I met him, most of those years were well behind him. I moved to Harrison, Arkansas in 1973 to work as a Naturalist at the newly formed Buffalo National Park. Clyde was the county clerk there, and one of the best liked, well respected men I have ever known. Everyone in the county liked him and trusted him. I was in my early 20s and trying to learn everything I could about turkey hunting. I couldn't have found a better teacher.

I pestered Clyde for all his turkey hunting secrets and he kept telling me that if I would stick with it, the wild gobblers I hunted would teach me better than all the veterans and all the books and all the seminars in the world. Truer words were never spo-

The secret formula to success never changes. There are two ingredients — patience and persistence.

ken.

I can tell you now what he had that made him such a great turkey hunter... it was pure and simple patience and persistence. He loved it so much it was easy for him to be sitting in the same place at noon where he had first settled at dawn. And as he so often said, "Good turkey callers don't kill turkeys, boy. Good hunters kill turkeys and good hunters can wait... poor hunters can't sit still."

I learned early that you didn't always have to wait. Sometimes a gobbler would run to the most mediocre call ever produced. Sometimes you could hit a foul note or two and still bag a tom in 15 minutes. But more times than not, the most perfect calling you ever heard isn't what you need to bag a bird. You have to know the wild turkey, you have to know where and how to set up and you have to learn something about patience. And about the only thing that breeds patience is confidence gained from experience.

In the spring of 1995, I was going after my 70th gobbler and I remember thinking about Clyde that morning as I left my house to hike a mile or so back into the woods where several gobblers had been roosting and rambling for most of the winter.

I still wasn't near the hunter he had been and I knew it.

I had killed 69 gobblers over the past 23 years because of great opportunities... several states to hunt in, increasing numbers of turkeys and increasing season lengths and bag limits. By the 1980s, Missouri had a two bird limit and Arkansas allowed three toms per season. Between the two states, a hunter could hunt for five weeks, from the end of March into May. There were several years in which I took a total of five gobblers from the Ozark mountains of Missouri and Arkansas during the spring because my profession as an outdoor writer gave me lots of time to hunt.

Every time I did something wrong a wild gobbler let me know about it. I learned by hunting them just how well they can see and hear and over the years I discovered that most hunters fail because they use mouth calls which are just too loud, not understanding at all just how far away a gobbler can hear that call. And finally, I learned a little bit about patience. Soon it became obvious that success in turkey hunting is directly related to the amount of time a hunter can spend on the seat of his pants and how well he can remain hidden.

Hiding of course, is another important part of the equation. Sometimes beginning hunters hide too well. I remember how Clyde laughed when I told him about getting way back in a multiflora rose thicket and spending an hour trying to see a tom which gobbled around me only 20 yards away. I had hidden so well I had no chance to kill the turkey. I couldn't see anything but the thicket around me. Most hunters don't hide well enough, of course, not understanding the vision of a wild turkey. I've convinced myself over the years that a gobbler within 50 yards can see your eyes move and blink.

Many times I've been in the woods and walked up on some hunter who I saw a hundred yards away. If I could see him so easily, he certainly wasn't hidden well enough. Of course you can't tell anyone how to conceal themselves, that's an art you have to learn. Wild gobblers taught me a lot about that over the years too. Clyde advised me to never set in the sunlight. Stay in the shadows and if there's no eye-high vegetation between you and the gobbler, cut a few small limbs quickly and stick them up around you. Two other things will get you a few gobblers over the years which you otherwise would have lost... a camouflaged shotgun and a face mask.

That morning in April of 1995, I quickly found my gobblers sounding off on the roost in a hollow before me. I hope you're up there somewhere watching, Clyde, 'cause down in that hollow, gobbler number 70 is wrapping his toes around a limb for the last time, I said to myself. Of course, saying it is one thing and believing it is something else.

I set up on a timbered hilltop above them, next to an old field dotted with buckbrush and multi-flora rose. One tom answered me a time or two on the ground and then it was over for quite some time. About 6:30 I peered over the buckbrush out into that field and there they were. The two mature gobblers were in full strut in the midst of seven hens, a good 150 yards across the clearing. In all the years of hunting turkeys I've never seen the same thing happen twice. Each dawning day is a new story. Every time I watch a strutting gobbler on a bright April morning, it feels like I'm seeing it for the first time and I realize all over again that sometimes the greatest rewards for a hunter has nothing to do with squeezing the trigger.

Mating hens usually pick a gobbler and crouch submissively before him, but that morning none of the hens in the field were interested in mating. They ambled here and there, feeding out of the field, then back into it. A third gobbler came in from the timber across from me and the two strutting toms ran him off in short order. All this time I was calling softly with my little homemade box call, thinking I had probably kept the worst of the 10 or 15 I had made and given the best ones away. Whistling the national anthem would have produced no less results. But experience told me those two gobblers had heard every sound I had made. They just didn't care.

Then suddenly there were only three hens left and they headed back into the area where they had roosted with the strutting toms behind them as if drawn on a string. And then they were gone and I stood there thinking it would be smart to go somewhere else and start over again with a more receptive gobbler.

I mustered as much patience as I could, and stayed and stayed and stayed... for a good 30 minutes. I think I would have waited another 30 minutes or so before searching for greener pastures, but to tell the truth, I had no confidence in seeing those two gobblers again. Still, gobblers from years past had taught me it was likely that I would. I kept calling every now and then to stay warm, but the field looked awfully empty.

But then, the miracle. Back out in the field and a hundred yards away, over the top of a little rise, I glimpsed a bobbing red and white head and then marching into full view, a black-bodied tom followed by another, no longer strutting, but stepping it off at a brisk pace. I sank low against the big oak and called one more time. They were only about 60 yards away when I brought my shotgun up and each seemed afraid the other would get there first. Apparently the hens had abandoned them and they had the appearance of two guys who had taken their dates home early and were heading back to town. Both had full beards, so I tried to pick out the biggest, but there wasn't much time to make a decision. I pulled the trigger when the gobblers were 20 yards away and still coming far enough apart so I wouldn't drop them both. The tom dropped in his tracks, flopping around in his death throes while the other gobbler ran in a circle around him before flying off into the adjacent timber. The beard was full and long, but I paid more attention to the long, sharp spurs when I

He had seven beards which ran ranged from five inches to 11 and totaled 50 inches or better. I always wondered how many his partner had.

placed my tag on his leg. Minutes later I was headed for home with the gobbler over my shoulder, wondering why he didn't weigh more. Across that field he had looked to be 25 pounds. At home, he weighed only 20 pounds, with 1 and 1/4 inch spurs, probably a three year old tom. But when I looked closer at the beard, an hour or so later, I got the surprise of my life. There were seven of them. The main beard was 11 inches long, the rest of them about six or seven inches in length, and thin. But still, there were seven distinguishable beards about an inch or so apart all the way up the breast.

Until then I had never killed a multi-bearded gobbler. I had seen a few. In fact, a year before I was fishing on Bull Shoals lake in late April when I found a nice-sized wild turkey with four beards floating dead in a remote cove. I think he had been scared off the roost in the night and flew into a bluff on the lake. I remember Clyde talking about bagging toms with two or three beards, but nothing close to seven.

I know the Wild Turkey Federation has a scoring system for wild turkeys, and several people have mentioned to me that the seven-bearded gobbler would have ranked high on that list. But I have never believed in making trophies out of wildlife, it is of little interest to me. In years past, hunters in several areas of the country have made efforts to get their names in those "record books" by feeding and baiting turkeys.

If you are hunting gobblers for recognition, you are hunting for the wrong reason and you're missing something. That morning hunt was one I will always remember, but just as exciting were those hunts when the gobblers were smaller and with shorter beards and spurs. I've killed bigger toms, and older birds, gobblers with longer spurs. The wildest gobblers I've hunted are the ones deep in the national forests of Arkansas and those birds seldom weigh more than 20 pounds. They are turkeys of a darker color with very dark brown bands on the tail and beards which seem to be thinner. These wild turkeys are in areas where there have not been domestic turkeys to cross with, nor any introduced strains from other areas. The larger the gobbler, the more likely it is to stem from turkeys which have some domestic blood. So it seems a little silly to be boasting about the size of a gobbler, or how highly he might "score." Spur length tells you something of his age, and when you see spurs which are longer than 1 and 1/4 inches, you've fooled a bird that has probably seen several spring seasons and heard a few turkey calls in years past. It seems that I learned a little more from the experience with each one of them.

That seven bearded gobbler was my 70th gobbler and even he taught me something. But it doesn't take 70 gobblers to teach you what it takes to be an effective turkey hunter — your first one can teach you that. Forget the greener woods on the other side of the fence. Get out there at dawn and get swallowed up in the timber. Find a spot and convince yourself it's the best place in the world to hunt gobblers... and let some old hesitant tom that's slower than ice-box molasses teach you a little bit about patience.

Chapter Nine

"Shootin' Buzzards off a Dead Cow"

Mike Dodson grew up in the Ozark hills of north Arkansas, in a family of hunters. He was about as good at it as anyone I've ever met, one of those people who just naturally has a feel for the woods and a built in comprehension of the ways of the wild. But in the beginning, he didn't know a thing about wild turkeys. He and I started hunting ducks together in the early 1980s, and fortunately for him, I decided to teach him everything I knew about wild gobblers.

It was the least I could do. One year, just before the spring season opened, Mike volunteered to take me down to a secret hunting spot of his where he had hunted deer in the fall since he was a youngster. It was a prime spot for turkeys as well, way back in the National Forest south of the Buffalo River. We hiked back to a little saddle where he said he had seen a few turkeys in the past and I stopped and hooted like a barred owl. Around us, four or five gobblers opened up. My old buddy had taken me to

a veritable turkey hunters heaven. Now all I had to do was get rid of him and figure out how to get back there.

The first part was easy. Poor old Mike had to work on the first morning of the season. Rich Abdoler, another one of our duck hunting friends, came down to camp with me and we pitched a tent back in the middle of Mike's old deer hunting grounds. On opening day, I called up a nice gobbler and killed it about 7:00 a.m., so I returned to camp and fixed breakfast. In Arkansas back then, you could kill two gobblers in a season in the Ozarks and then add a third one by going down south of the Arkansas river to hunt in the Ouachita's. You could hunt all day and take two gobblers in one day if you were so lucky. And that day, I was lucky. About 10:00 or so that morning I had another gobbler going as I sat on an old logging road halfway up the side of a mountain about a half mile from camp. And he was coming to me, slowly but surely, when I began to hear a weird droning sound. It didn't take long to figure out what it was. The motor of an A.T.V. moved down the old trail and then stopped. Then there was the loud

When Mike Dodson went turkey hunting, no gobbler was safe, no matter how high the mountain or deep the canyon. If it took him all day, he'd get to that tom, and he'd be there 'til the sun went down.

mournful yelp of a diaphragm mouth call. The guy on the A.T.V. had heard my gobbler and he was going after him. The gobbler shut up and the motor started again. Moments later he came bouncing along, and stopped beside me.

"I heard one down in here somewhere," he said, "You hear 'im too?"

I lied and said I hadn't, but I think he knew better. He fired up his motorized legs and whined on past me. I waited and sure enough in about 30 minutes here he came back, wanting to know if I had heard that gobbler again. This time I said I hadn't, and this time I wasn't lying. He rode off back up the old road the way he had come, off to try to find another gobbler he could call without having to walk far from his four-wheeler. I lay back in the leaves and took a nap, saying a little prayer that I would never get so lazy or so out-of-shape that I had to hunt turkeys on an A.T.V

I was awakened just after noon by that gobbler again, about where he was two hours before. By 1:00 p.m. I had him gobbling about 35 yards away. I wondered, while the sound of the shotgun blast echoed across the valley, if the old boy on the A.T.V. was close enough to hear the shot with his motor running.

Rich Abdoler killed a turkey that afternoon

and we took them back to Harrison, where Mike is a city fireman, and showed them to him. He turned all sorts of shades of green, and said he was awful happy for us. He said he'd be off work on Wednesday, and he meant to go out and try his hand at gobbler hunting for the first time.

Of course I saw that as an opportunity and I felt like I owed Mike the chance to bag a gobbler on his own. We headed back to camp on Tuesday evening and at first light the next morning we were standing on a high peak where an old rock wall remained from a homestead perhaps a hundred years old. Surrounded by forest, we were so far back in those mountains it didn't seem possible that someone could have actually lived there in a different century and tried to scratch out a living in such a wild and primitive land. But the kind of people that did just that were Mike Dodson's ancestors and that son-of-a-gun was as tough as any of them. He was a high school football star and in the summer softball league you always knew who was going to win it all... the team that had Mike Dodson. Mark McGuire had nothing on him. If Mike didn't hit one or two over the fence every game it was because he was home sick.

I think that morning I made some feeble attempt to talk Mike into playing for our team in the upcoming summer. He said I was one of the best duck hunters he knew, but possibly the very worst softball manager in the whole north part of Arkansas. With me pitching, he figured even he couldn't help the team. But he'd play for me, he said with a grin, if I could call up a pair of gobblers for him before noon. He said it with a sort of fat-chance-of-that attitude. My feelings were hurt just a little, but I had to admit he was right about the duck hunting part of it.

I shrugged it off and pulled out my turkey call, and as the morning approached, we found ourselves just uphill from a whole flock of gobblers. Several of them shook the dew from the new buds around us with their answer to my call. We quickly set up back from the rock wall, and in 30 minutes four or five turkeys came popping up over the edge of the steep hill, still gobbling as they came. I don't know which of those were big ones and which were little ones and Mike didn't care. He leveled off at a red head and squeezed off a round, then crossed that rock wall like a Confederate officer at Gettysburg. His gobbler was flopping down the hill and Mike went after him, leaving his gun behind. About 15 minutes later he climbed up out of there with a jake across his shoulder and his elbows bleeding. He looked worse than the young gobbler he had retrieved, but there was a smile across his face that said Mike would be a turkey hunter for life.

Late in the morning, he took me to another place where he had hunted deer as a kid and we walked again down an old logging road, picking out a good spot to call from. There wasn't a gobble to be heard, but we sat down, Mike on one side of a big oak and me on the other and I began to call. We hadn't been there 15 minutes when a hen came walking past me, putting and perking in low tones. I was watching her when I heard Mike's shotgun go off behind me and I swear I thought he had shot at the hen. But there was another turkey on Mike's side, another jake which hadn't gobbled, or made a sound. The lucky rascal had killed two toms before noon on his very first turkey hunt.

We packed up camp that afternoon and headed home with Mike on cloud nine. He relived the whole experience over and over, until finally there was a pause and just a moment or two of silence.

"Mike," I said, "where do you want to play?"

He was quiet for a moment with a puzzled look on his face. So I continued.

"You know... on our softball team." I repeated, "What position would you like to play?"

Never has a successful turkey hunter with his head in the clouds come crashing back to earth so quickly. And what's even more amazing, the upcoming week-end we journeyed down to the Ouachita mountains and on the first morning there, Mike killed another gobbler which I called in. Back in Harrison, he showed the beards of his three turkeys to his uncle Jack, a fine experienced hunter who had spent the first week without firing a shot. And he just had to rub it in a little. "Just like shootin' buzzards off a dead cow," he told his uncle, "...like shootin' buzzards off a dead cow."

The whole thing didn't sit well with uncle Jack Dodson, who just nodded and told Mike that he'd live to regret saying that. And sure enough, there were seasons to come when the younger hunter would have his difficulties. But Jack underestimated his nephew. Mike learned to call turkeys that summer and because of his strength and woodsmanship, he continued to have great success. If Mike heard a turkey in the Grand canyon, he would figure out a way to get there and he would stay with him till he bagged him. No gobbler, no matter how far away he was, or how inaccessible that mountain terrain seemed, was safe if Mike got a bearing on him.

Within a few years we began to guide turkey hunters in the spring, in Arkansas and southern Missouri. For several years we sacrificed much of the turkey season to take others who didn't have much experience. This was in the 1980s, when turkey numbers were high everywhere. We'd usually set up a base camp somewhere and take a pair of doctors or surgeons or lawyers after their first gobblers. And most of the time we were successful.

Toward the end of the season one year, Mike and I had a couple of days to hunt on our own and we got off down into the Ozark mountains just south of Jasper, Arkansas where it was so rough we knew it hadn't been hunted. Up until then, I had felt about the same age as Mike Dodson, but that was the year I began to realize he was quite a bit younger than me and I was quite a bit smarter. One morning we stood on a high peak, peering down into a chasm which

Mike Dodson and I with the two gobblers we killed together on top of an Ozark mountain... hours after a futile hike to the bottom of the canyon where we first heard them.

looked two miles deep and Mike was chomping at the bit to see the bottom of it.

Of course there was a reason for his enthusiasm. We were hearing what sounded like four distinct gobblers in that bottomless pit. And experience told me I could call them up out of there, while his exuberance told him it would be more fun to join them in that creek bed. He could have been right. I was pretty sure there were hens with them — they might never come up out of there if the hens didn't come first. And if they didn't want to climb a mountain, they had to go up or down that creek. We had a 50-50 chance of being where they would go, even if we didn't call.

And so, we did it. We walked up the ridge aways and pitched off down into that abyss, using our elbows for brakes and doing a great deal more sliding than stepping. We had calculated things pretty well... when we reached the bottom we were at least 150 yards upstream from the flock and I'm pretty sure we were looking at a little spot in the wilderness where no white man had ever set foot before. Maybe no Indians either, for that matter. The setting was absolutely beautiful, with giant hardwoods and a lush undergrowth with spring flowers growing around giant boulders and a clear cold mountain stream rushing past. I gave a passing thought to timber rattlers and then shrugged it off. We had more serious problems to think of than timber rattlers. I remembered right then, the time a mouse got in my trash can in the basement workshop and how I watched him try valiantly to scale the side of that barrel. He'd get about two-thirds of the way up it, then fall back to the bottom. As impossible as it was for him to scale the side of that trash can, imagine how hard it would have been for him to climb out with a little gun on his back and cockroach slung over his shoulder. Now you know what kind of predicament we were in should we have killed a gobbler.

But then again, there wasn't a thing to keep us from staying down in that little oasis and enjoying the morning calling gobblers. We got set up and sent forth some seductive calling and didn't hear a thing. Not a gobble, not a yelp, not a putt... not a thing except the sound of rushing water. So eventually we moved off to the side and up the opposite bank a little where we could hear better and we called some more. And that's when we heard it — a double gobble, clear and deep, echoing off the walls of that canyon, wafting down from a spot high on the mountain above... where we had been only an hour or so before.

I guess that was one of the low points in a long

friendship. But we were in it together and the only way out was to climb the side of that mountain. I knew that when and if I made it up out of there I would be a better man for it. If not, surely there would eventually be a search party and a helicopter. It was a slow and torturous ordeal and I'm almost positive that if I hadn't had a sling on my shotgun I would have had to leave it in that canyon. But in the end, when it was all said and done, we crawled over the edge and onto level ground. I felt like one of those Sherpa tribesmen as I lay there gazing into a clear blue sky filled with the last few dogwood blossoms of the spring.

The rest of the story is sort of anti-climatic. The gobblers were only about 100 yards away and we heard them even before we called. We set up about 10 or 15 yards apart and sat there for the better part of two hours trying to get them in range. It wasn't so much of a job to be patient that morning. Exhaustion, skinned knees and inflamed joints make it easier to sit back and wait. About noon, the whole flock sidled over toward us and sure enough there were several hens, two or three jakes and one big old gobbler. When they began to inch toward us and forage for acorns at the edge of shotgun range, the old gobbler strutted a little, and took the lead. He was mine, I knew. Mike and I had long ago developed a system in which, should we call in two gobblers while hunting together, he took the one on his side and I took the one on mine. The big tom was in the lead and that was on my side. Finally, they were inside 40 yard and I gave a quiet little call with my mouth. It was a dumb thing to do. Two of the jakes came running up past the monarch, putting both of them in my line of fire. They had scarcely attained that position when Mikes shotgun roared and the big gobbler went down. There was little else for me to do but flatten one of the jakes, so I did it.

We didn't get back to the pick-up for hours and by the time we got there I had already vowed to try to find me one of those A.T.V.s somewhere. I had begun to think of relaxing somewhere over a crappie bed, watching a bobber, and I certainly was skeptical about ever returning to those mountains again. But as time goes on, you forget about the bad times and remember the good. That mouse back home in the basement which I had released, I knew he'd be back in that trash can again if I dropped an apple core in it. Turkey hunters are a lot like that.

In very little time we were bouncing along a gravel road in my old pick-up, when uncle Jack came past us. We pulled over and stopped and exchanged greetings. For once, Mike's uncle got in the first word.

"I got a pretty nice one this morning," he told us.

"I'll tell you, they are roosting down in those deep valleys and spending the morning down in the low ground along the creeks, but if you'll wait they'll come up on the ridges eventually."

"You know," Mike said reflectively, as we pulled away before uncle Jack had really even finished telling us about his gobbler. "You learn something new every day."

Right then, I would have liked to have wrung his neck.

Chapter Ten

Jakes

*T*here will be those years when turkey hunting isn't up to par and we've had a few of them in the mid-1990's. During that period, we had some pretty poor hatches in our region. Two years after a poor nesting season, hunters notice that it's much tougher than it ought to be to call in a gobbler. That's because the two-year-old gobblers aren't very plentiful and it's the two-year-olds that respond best to a call. Two-year-old gobblers are prime for mating, but get kicked around pretty good by the older toms. Dominant gobblers are the three- and four-year-old toms and they are slower to come to a call for several reasons. They are usually warier because of age and stronger. They win the fights and they get the hens. And while plenty of them will fall to hunters guns, they will be harder to bring into range. Two-year-olds are desperate for love and easier to fool. When there are lots of those younger gobblers, hunting is good.

According to my unofficial observations, during normal years, the two-year-olds make up about 50

or 60 percent of the harvest, jakes make up 15 or 20 percent and older gobblers make up the rest. When you are hunting in the spring and you see lots of the jakes, you figure the following spring will afford some pretty good turkey hunting. Jakes of course, are the almost-one-year-old turkeys which have small bumps where the spurs will be and beards about three or four inches long. When you've hunted turkeys for awhile, you'll be able to tell the difference in a mature gobbler and a jake just by looking. Jakes look long legged and gawky because of more slender bodies and if you ever see one strutting, the tail feathers will be uneven when fanned, longer in the center and shorter to each side.

I think there will be quite a difference in jakes hatched early, say in late May or June and jakes hatched late in the summer, but that's not backed up by any scientific facts, its just my own observations. A two-year-old gobbler may actually weigh 22 to 24 pounds and it seems that the older birds start to decline in weight, perhaps because the stress of breeding and fighting takes away some size. You see jakes with really significant weight differences taken in the

---

Jakes may not be quite as hard to call and kill as the old gobblers, but they aren't pushovers. They have a long-legged, and somewhat awkward look but when they gobble and strut they deserve to be carried home over a hunter's shoulder.

same areas, some up to 18 pounds and others only 13 or 14 pounds.

I have killed a number of jakes in my time and the ones which gobble and act like mature gobblers are usually up in that 18 pound range in Missouri, 15 or 16 pounds in the Arkansas mountains. You may be ashamed of killing a jake in the spring, but if one gobbles and responds to your call, he's worth hunting. Sure, most of us would rather take a big old ground-raker with spurs an inch and a half long, but there are times when I've been disappointed by those old-timers.

Many years ago I was hunting in Arkansas near the headwaters of the Big Piney river which flows southward into the Arkansas river. It's rough country and you can hike back into areas where few hunters ever go, places where there are timber rattlers and black bear and natural beauty of astounding pro-portions. It took all morning to get back into the mid-dle of where I wanted to be and I hadn't heard any gobblers along the way. When I'm hunting in those vast forestlands down in Arkansas, I like to find an old logging road or a long ridge-top and just walk and call, stopping for 10 or 15 minutes to wait and listen, then move on for aways and repeat the procedure. That kind of hunting is enjoyable for me because I get to see so much new country and as the day goes on, you get to places few people hunt. When a gobbler responds, you have all day to work him and no one to interfere.

That's what happened that day that back in the 1980s. I found an old spring-fed pond on top of a ridge where there had been a cabin maybe a hundred years ago, with nothing remaining but a rock foundation and fireplace. There were some bear tracks in the soft ground around that small pothole and I was looking them over when I thought I heard a gobble in the valley below me. So I got myself situated in heavy woods above the old home place where I could see well and stay hidden and I began to call. Finally I heard a clear, distinct gobble down in that valley and my heart jumped. Who could ask for a better situation.

An hour later I was eating my lunch and had pretty much given up on hearing that turkey again. He hadn't made a sound. I packed things away in my backpack and stood up and when I did I saw the gobbler standing on a shelf just beneath me, about 40 yards away. Somehow, he had failed to see me. A split second later I had my sights on him and as the shotgun blast echoed across the valley, he went down for the count. That was probably the oldest turkey I'll ever kill. His spurs were an inch and a half long and sharp as daggers. And he was one of the most beautiful gobblers I've ever seen, with a short tail, probably two inches shorter than many of the Missouri gobblers I've killed, and rimmed with a dark chocolate band darker than any I had ever seen, which is typical of the true strain wild turkeys which were once found in the Midwest before domestic turkeys came in and began to dilute the genetics. I didn't get him back to weigh him until late in the evening, but that old-timer only weighed about 17 pounds. If he would have weighed 25 pounds, I don't know if I would have made it back.

Contrast that with the first wild turkey I ever killed, back when I was just learning to hunt gobblers. I had chased them for most of a week and the season was nearly over. But a new day dawned clear and calm and at sunrise, I had a gobbler on a ridge across from me sounding off every time I hit the call. When he flew off the roost, he pitched down into the valley below me and must have gobbled 50 times only 150 yards away.

I hid myself pretty well that morning and sat there shaking with excitement, calling with a new box call I had found the evening before. Boy that gobbler loved it. He would gobble every time I would call and sometimes when I wouldn't. When it became apparent he was slowly inching his way up that hillside toward me, I brought my old 97 Winchester to my shoulder and tried to guess where he might appear. And he made it easy because he just kept gobbling as he came. When that blood red head appeared in the undergrowth before me, my hands were shaking so badly I could scarcely hold the barrel still enough to aim. Then he stepped out into the open, huffed up as if to break into a strut and gave forth a gobble that shook the spring buds around me. I bowled him over with one shot and there was so much adrenaline in me that when I went to look over my very first gobbler I ran past him 20 or 30 feet and had to come back to find him. He was a beige-tailed turkey which most likely had one or two of his ancestors originating from an Ozark homestead some years back, because he also weighed 18 and 1/2 pounds. Which of those two gobblers do you think made the most exciting hunt. I'll never pass up a Jake which provides that kind of a morning.

Another Jake I'll always remember was one that weighed only 16 or 17 pounds which my 14 year old daughter killed in the Ozark mountains of Arkansas near the headwaters of the Buffalo river. Christy had begged me to take her hunting with me since she was way too small to go. In fact, she and her mother went on a trip with me in Missouri one year when she was only about seven or eight years old. It was the opening morning and I sat the two of them down be-

My daughter Christy with her mother, Gloria, with the biggest gobbler I ever bagged, a 26 pounder. It was my daughters first turkey hunt.

hind me and began to call a gobbler in the valley below us. The plan was, I'd call the turkey in close and let Christy and Gloria get a good look at it, then let it pass by unharmed. Back then, in the late 1970s, there were lots of gobblers and I didn't want to kill one the first morning. I intended to wait that year for a real ground-raker. Things never happen the way you think it will. The gobbler came up to us in only 45 minutes or so and shook the leaves with it's gobbles only 30 or 40 yards away on the other side of a thicket. Christy had never been on a turkey hunt and she was a little spooked by it. She asked her mother in a whisper, "Mama, if daddy doesn't get it, can he hurt us?" Her eyes must have been as big as saucers when that gobbler stepped out into the open, strutting, blowing and gobbling. So were mine. It was a huge tom, I sup-

At the age of 14, Christy killed her first gobbler in the Arkansas Ozarks. It was a hefty 17 pound jake which gobbled before her as she lifted her gun.

pose the biggest I have ever seen within range. I couldn't pass that gobbler up and Christy was delighted when we tagged him together. He weighed 26 pounds. the heaviest I've ever taken.

When she was 14 years old, Christy got her chance at a big tom one morning in the Arkansas mountains. We sat down above several turkeys sounding off on a bench below us and they came up to the call slowly but surely. Two jakes topped the edge of the bench and I could see a mature gobbler strutting about twenty yards behind them. But the jakes were all Christy could see and they both gobbled 30 yards before her. She flattened one of them and for the first time in my life, I couldn't have cared less about the size of a beard or the spurs. What a day to remember.

Remember that there's no shame in taking a jake which responds to your call gobbling and strutting as many of them will. You might be ashamed of hunting gobblers with a decoy or shooting one off the roost, or baiting one when you feel extra desperate, but calling up a gobbler is calling up a gobbler, even if it isn't an old ground-raker.

However, should you ever get to a point where you are something of a local turkey hunting legend and have reputation to uphold and should you accidentally wind up with a jake gobbler that looks as it he might have been looking for his mama rather than a girlfriend, here's a list of excuses which some of my hunting buddies have used in the past when they've brought a jake to the check station:

Excuse #1   He came up behind me and gobbled. I shot him because of quick reflexes.

Excuse #2 I'm going to have company the rest or the week and can't hunt any more.

Excuse #3   I feel like I'm coming down with the flu and may not get to hunt any more this week.

Excuse #4 I shot at a big tom and the jake ran in front of him as I pulled the trigger.

Excuse #5   The fishing is really getting good and I need to concentrate on bass and crappie.

Excuse #6 He attacked my dog... attacked my hunting partner... attacked me... (substitute whatever fits.)

Excuse #7   I hate to eat those old birds because they are so tough... rather bag a young one every year because the meat's so tender.

Excuse #8 Found him dead and didn't want to see him wasted (this is the old "Dedicated Conservationist" line).

Excuse #9   Wanted to spend more time with the family this week, (Wife put her foot down about some work around the house).

Excuse #10 Tired of ticks, wet feet and poison ivy and never want to hear another alarm clock at 4:30 a.m.

It's better, I suppose to use one of these excuses than the ones you have to come up with when the season is half over and you haven't got one yet.

Chapter Eleven

Slower Than Cold Molasses

My younger sister married an Arkansas boy without even consulting me and for a long time I thought she had made a mistake. I changed my mind when I found out he liked to hunt and fish. Billy Chadwick became a Missouri Highway Patrolman in 1975 and about that time we began to hunt turkeys together in southern Missouri. I could see the value in having a brother-in-law in the Highway patrol. I called up a lot of gobblers for Billy in those early years and I have no idea how many trees he shot during that time. But he also killed a lot of toms and finally learned how to do it himself and hasn't had a whole lot to do with me since. After he stopped hunting with me and some of my buddies he worked up fairly quickly and became a captain somewhere in the Ozarks. I think I know where he's at, but he never has sent an address.

Back in the good old days, Billy helped me to extend the hunting season. If I should happen to get a gobbler the first day or so, I would offer to go

along and call him in a good one. He couldn't hardly say no and it was a good opportunity for me to practice my calling. If I already had my gobbler, the pressure was gone and I could try all the things a hunter might not do ordinarily. Believe me, there is no better way to learn how to call turkeys than to practice on real wild gobblers and if you are going to experiment, it is best to do that when you are calling turkeys for your brother-in-law or some other relative.

Many years ago, late in the season, Billy and I were walking along a timbered ridge. I was telling him how I had killed my gobbler and how sorry I was that he didn't have one, when low and behold, across a deep valley there was a distinct, clear gobble.

Normally it's difficult to call a tom off of one ridge across a valley to another ridge. But it was late in the morning and I figured that gobbler had been abandoned by the hen or hens he had been cavorting with

When he heard my call, faint though it must have been wafting across the valley, I'm sure he

---

Billy Chadwick, approching the dying gobbler which took us a whole morning to call in. We weren't that patient, we only stayed four hours because we were watching him the whole time. Seems like he came a mile.

thought he recognized it... some sweet young hen from a past spring perhaps. And there are always those gobblers you'll remember which run to your call as if they are being pulled on a string. There won't be many, but everyone who hunts much, will remember a few of them. Those are the gobblers that convince you of your calling ability. You'll go out the next time absolutely confident that you are a champion turkey caller and then you encounter a gobbler which won't budge.

The turkey Billy and I encountered late in the morning way back there in the late '70s was a runner. He was out to get a hen of his very own and he didn't mind crossing a small valley to do it. We could hear him moving down the ridge in a hurry into the creek bottom gobbling about every eight or 10 steps. This, I decided, was a time to experiment with the old call.

So I began calling rapidly and often. I cackled, whined, clucked, purred, yelped and pleaded, in high gear. Surely, if all the old veterans were right this gobbler would hesitate and reconsider. But he crossed that valley like Sherman crossed Georgia and came rushing into shotgun range with reckless abandon.

Billy let him get about 40 yards away... then ended it all with a load of number four magnums. The tom went down hard and flopped around for quite some time as most of them do. We couldn't have known that apparently the gobbler was only grazed somehow. My brother-in-law tagged the bird and then we headed for the pickup, each of us complimenting the other on how well we had done and how well the gobbler had done.

Suddenly the bird began to come back to life, flogging and spurring my brother-in-law violently in an attempt to regain his freedom. Billy dropped the 20-pound tom and to our amazement he got his feet beneath him and began hotfooting it for the nearby valley. Fortunately, there was a shell left in my brother-in-law's shotgun magazine and he let the gobbler get no farther than 30 yards.

Now, I've never before seen a wild gobbler running through the woods with a hunter's tag around his leg. We wondered later what another hunter might have thought if he had called up a tom with Billy's tag on its leg. It would have created an interesting situation. He could have taken the number and returned the bird to the hunter who killed it first, or he could have kept it and said nothing.

He could not, however, make anyone else believe it. I'm sure I'm not doing real well at making some folks believe such a thing could really happen, but it did. Of course I know there's some doubt as to whether the wobbly-legged gobbler would have survived, but there's no doubt my brother-in-law would never have caught him on foot. He seemed to be gaining momentum and was just about ready to take to flight.

I told Billy that he shouldn't have shot the turkey that second time. I could have called him back again in short order, I assured him. There was nothing pressing about the situation. Granted, it would have taken 30 minutes or so to do it, but it would have been another good turkey to practice on with my call. To tell the truth, I don't really think I could have done it, but you never know. It's surprising what you can do when you experiment.

And though that all sounds like a tall story, it isn't. It happened just exactly as I have told it. But there was another hunt Billy and I were a part of back in the early 1980s which was even more remarkable to me. We were hunting on private land near the small community of Tyrone in south-central Missouri. I was born not far from there near the community of Yukon, in Texas county. If you've never heard of Tyrone or Yukon, I don't know how you'll ever make a turkey hunter.

Anyway it was another one of those situations where I had killed a gobbler and was trying to help Billy fill his tag. And for the first two hours that morning we heard very little. So we walked around over some new ground and called and listened and waited and walked. Eventually we ended up on a small creek with some pasture. It's difficult to describe the lay of the land, but one long field lay before us and it rose into a hillside. The field ended at the top of that hill and I am sure it was almost 3/4 of a mile across it. But under some big trees at the end of that field, up at the top of the hill there were three turkeys and you couldn't tell if they were hens or toms, just that they were turkeys The little handmade box calls I use are not very loud and there was some wind that day. I figured there wasn't a chance in the world those turkeys could hear us, but I called to them as loud as I could and you could see one of the three begin to strut. We situated ourselves in the little creek so that we could watch them without being seen and I nearly wore that little box out, calling loud and often. And little by little, slowly and surely, the three gobblers began moving down that hillside, all three strutting a little and gobbling, I could tell by their actions. But in the wind and at that distance, we couldn't hear them.

We sat there, fairly well hidden and watched those three gobblers move slowly down the sloping field, apparently responding to my call. By 10:00 a. m. they had reached the creek bottom and were about half as far as they had been when we first saw

If you could watch all your gobblers the way we watched those toms that morning, you would put your tag on most of them... eventually.

them. We could now see they were all mature gobblers and all three would strut a little. But one was obviously the dominant tom and he was the only one that was gobbling. When he would move toward one of the other toms, that one would stop strutting and get out of his way. Even in the strong wind, they were still hearing us, several hundred yards away. I would have bet they would not be able to hear my quiet little box call that far away. We really learned something about a turkey's sense of hearing that day.

But they were coming to us, slowly but surely

and it looked as if it would just be a matter of time. Time however, could be a problem. In Missouri back then, hunters had to leave the woods at noon. Would they make it in range by then? Four or five intruders made it less likely. Out of the woods near the three gobblers came a couple of hens and several jakes and they all began to mingle in the field. I figured a fight would break out and sure enough it did. One of the three old gobblers jumped on one of the jakes and flogged him pretty good, causing the three younger gobblers to move out to the perimeter, where they stood gawking around like teen-aged farm boys at their first dance. The hens joined the big gobblers and then there was a fight between the three of them. All this took a half hour or so and in

*Time can be a problem — hunters have to leave
the woods early... gobblers don't.*

the end, the hens left with the jakes, heading back into the woods and the three gobblers continued to strut in the middle of the field, now uninterested in my call. I think they were expecting the hens to return. Billy and I were watching the clock, knowing that if the gobblers ever did get within range, it was likely to be well after shooting hours ended. So we developed a plan. The creek bed we were in was nearly dry, with a few puddles and potholes here and there. But it curved around the edge of that field to about the edge of the woodland where the hens and jakes had emerged and at that point, a hunter would be within about 100 yards of the three toms. From where we were, they were perhaps three times that far.

The plan was simple and should work with no problem. Billy would take my turkey call, sneak around the creek bed down below the level of the field and completely hidden, until he had worked himself to that closer position and then he would call the gobblers over and uncap the head of the largest one. I would wait where I was with no call and no gun and root for him. It should have worked so well, but then come to think of it, when does anything work the way it's suppose to.

In the 15 or 20 minutes it took my brother-in-law to get where he wanted to get, those three gobblers remembered where they had been going in the first place and started coming right to me. When Billy looked up over the edge of the field, there were his three gobblers almost to where he had been and a long way from where he was. He could see he had to get back there in a hurry and that's what he did. Meanwhile, I crouched there and watched the big gobblers move to within about 40 yards, still gobbling and strutting. It was nearly noon and these turkeys which we had first seen as black dots on a distant hillside were finally right there where we had wanted them and my hunting partner had moved himself to a place where he couldn't possibly get one.

But all those years of teaching him finally paid off. He did just about as good as he could have done in that situation.

Rather than trying to get back to where I waited, he came back down the creek about halfway and began to call. I could faintly hear that calling and when I peered up over the edge of the field, the one big dominant gobbler was strutting away from me toward the spot where Billy was waiting. The other two were just standing and watching.

I looked down at my watch and it was about three minutes until noon. About that time I heard a shotgun blast and I ducked down to wait, just in case there was a need to shoot again. When I finally did rise to my feet there were no turkeys in the field except the big tom, flopping around about 40 yards from where Billy was trying to get out of the creek bottom thicket he had been hiding in. It had been a long shot, but he had made it and just in the nick of time. I got out in the field and took a few pictures as he approached the gobbler and congratulated him as he put his tag on the gobbler which took four hours to come to the call. If he had waited another 10 minutes in crossing that field he may have lived to become the prey of a roving bobcat on some cold winter night, or the victim of a bolt of lightning in a mid-summer storm.

And despite the fact that I had called that turkey for better than a half a mile and the best part of four hours, all Billy remembers is that he had the call during the last few minutes and to hear him tell it, he turned that old gobbler on a dime. I admitted he had done alright, but I told him in the future he should learn to pick a good spot and stay there rather than running up and down the creek like some dad-blamed greenhorn.

I never again watched a gobbler come that far to a call, or worked one nearly that long. But it convinced me that no one really knows how far away a gobbler can hear a call and I'm sure they can hear you farther than you can hear them.

We'd all probably kill more turkeys if we waited and waited and waited and never moved. Of course the skeptic could say that it's possible those gobblers would have done the same thing, chosen the same route and went the same direction that morning even if I hadn't been there calling. Could be, I guess, but skeptics make darn poor turkey hunters. As far as I'm concerned, we called them every step of the way. And come to think of it, three-quarters of a mile may have been a conservative estimate.

Chapter Twelve

A Letter To The Judge

$\mathcal{M}$ay 12, 1980

Dear Judge...

I really do appreciate the opportunity to write and give you my side of the story on this, since it's so doggone far to drive from Arkansas just to appear in court on something this silly. You see my brother-in-law is a highway patrolman up there in Missouri and actually he's the one who gave me that ridiculous ticket. Most folks would agree that going 61 in a 55 mile per hour zone shouldn't set a fellow back fifty-some dollars. You've got to understand, your honor, I'm an outdoor writer and that's more than I make sometimes in a whole week. Well, anyway this whole thing developed from last week's turkey season. You see, my brother-in-law who I have always thought the world of, even though I'm not sure he used good judgement in marrying my sister, well he

---

My brother-in-law, the highway patrolman, on the left, and my old hunting buddy John Green on the right. It must have been about 1981, the year after I wrote to the judge. Where and how the two of them bagged these gobblers we'll never know.

wanted to hunt gobblers and I agreed to take him. So I drove up from Arkansas with my old huntin' buddy John Green, who is just one heckuva guy but prone to a lot of joking around and cutting up and having a good time and maybe not as serious about things as I am. And we met my brother-in-law at my folks home on Sunday evening just before opening day. So I told him we had been stopped by a highway patrolman on the way up for going 95 miles per hour. Of course my brother-in-law, not knowing we were just pulling his leg, gets all concerned and I followed up by telling him the patrolman let us off because we gave him a couple of old Playboy magazines and a week-old Baby Ruth candy bar. Well we all had a good laugh and my brother-in-law seemed to think it was funny too... I mean he grinned a little even though he didn't say much. And let me say right here, your honor, that I have never even bought a Playboy magazine in my entire life and never do intend to. Outdoor Life is about the most liberal magazine I have in my old pick-up and I'd never think of offering one to a highway patrolman if I was going 95 miles per hour, which I never would be — and wasn't. Anyway the next day John and me both got a nice turkey and my brother-in-law didn't and I think that just throwed some more fat on the fire, especially when we found out my brother-in-law had called up a nice one and spooked him before he could get a shot. Not realizing how bad ol' Billy was feeling, we joked about how maybe he had developed a habit of jumping up and hollerin' Freeze, "turkey," you know how those cops do on the TV shows. Boy that went over like home-brew at the church picnic. That night my mom goes to bragging about how my brother-in-law makes up his bed before going hunting and me and John left ours as if we intended to come back and sleep awhile about mid-morning, which is exactly what we did intend to do of course. Well, just to have a little fun, while ol' Billy waited in the pick-up the next morning, I snuck back in and ruffled his bed up and poured some water on the sheets to make it look like he had wet the bed. Nothing but a little practical joke that me and John got one heck of a laugh out of later.

Well, as luck would have it ol' John and me called up a nice gobbler for my brother-in-law and he blowed the heck out of the tree the turkey stepped behind, and boy did we ever roll on the ground, holding our sides and sympathizing with him the best we knew how. But he did get a turkey your honor, the next morning, and I'd just as soon you didn't let my brother-in-law know I told you, but that little old jake didn't weigh 12 pounds on the heaviest scale we could find. John and me joked that he wasn't looking for a girl-friend when he heard our call. He was looking for his mama.

Anyway John and me thought it was all in good fun and we just had a heckuva good time until we got headed back to Arkansas. Of course my brother-in-law knew right when we'd be comin' through and he was waiting. When we saw those flashin' lights and recognized Ol' Billy, naturally we thought he was having some fun at our expense, but we didn't know what the expense was going to be. And so I'm hoping, your honor, that you are a turkey hunter too and might understand why this whole thing came about. I myself have always had the greatest respect for judges, whether they are the regular kind who hear murder trials and divorces or even those who have other jobs and still have to prescribe over these dad-blamed traffic tickets. And the book of Judges has always been one of my favorite books in the bible!

You might be interested to know that I have guided several judges on fishing trips all over the Ozarks and would be willing to take you on any trip you'd be interested in completely free, which is worth a good deal more than the measly $56 fine I'd have to pay for speeding.

And that brings me to that other little matter. Sure, I'll admit I did get out of my old pick-up with a 20 dollar bill in my hand that day but that wasn't anything close to bribery. I was just having a little fun with him... heck he's my very own brother-in-law. Of course judge, I'll go along with whatever you decide on this, but I hate to see a family broke all apart over a little bit of good-natured joking. I believe that boy could make a fine turkey hunter someday if I'm allowed to help him along.

Sincerely, Larry A. Dablemont

Chapter Thirteen
Hunting With a Dirty Rotten Skunk

I hunt and fish on occasion with a low-down, dirty, rotten skunk by the name of Jim Spencer. We were good friends once... before he did what he did. Well, to tell the whole story we were camped down in the Ouachita mountains of west Arkansas hunting wild turkeys, just me and him and Rich Abdoler. Spencer is an outdoor writer himself and to be fair, I'd have to say he's one of the best. When you read something Jim writes, you are captivated by it. He's one of the old-time writers who actually does what he writes about, unlike 99 per-cent of today's outdoor writers who live in city suburbs and do their fishing within six feet of a switch key and their hunting within six feet of a guide. Spencer works for the Arkansas Game and Fish Commission as a writer and free-lances in his spare time. No doubt he knows the outdoors, and you can see that when he writes about his experiences. That said, he is still prone to stretch the truth, and therefore isn't quite the same type of writer as I am.

Anyway we were camped down in the moun-

tains and he left his box of shotgun shells sitting on the table in camp the day before the season opened and went foraging around for mushrooms or something. So I emptied it of the shotshells and replaced them with half a brick that I had found nearby, a harmless little joke which I figured he'd catch onto long before daylight on opening day. That brick made the shell box feel almost exactly like it would feel if it was full of shells. It wasn't my fault that he tossed the box into his pick-up and drove off at dawn to his secret hunting spot. It wasn't my fault that when he heard the first gobbler he dug into his shell box and found a brick. And it wasn't my fault that the gobbler had shut up by the time he drove back to camp and found his shells and returned. It was a simple little joke and we all had a good laugh and forgot about it. Needless to say, I checked my sleeping bag every night and my shell box each morning before leaving camp. And then I sort of let my guard down, figuring my good friend had taken the joke in good humor and would let it go at that.

Two days later, Rich and I loaded my boat to go float the Fourche La Fave river, while Jim was off somewhere still chasing turkeys and carrying a grudge. A half mile down the stream I opened my tackle box to locate a favorite spinner-bait and found it's compart-

This low-down, dirty rotten skunk is my old friend Jim Spencer with a gobbler he shot in the Arkansas Ozarks and a string of fish he probably also shot in the Arkansas Ozarks.

ments filled with rocks and pine cones instead of lures. Then it hit me what a dirty, low-down, rotten skunk Jim Spencer was. I had to borrow a lure from Rich's skimpy tackle box and didn't catch a respectable fish the entire afternoon.

When we returned to camp, Jim was still gone, but there next to the tent, hanging from the long limb of a short-leaf pine was a rope made of my fishing lures, eight or nine feet of spinner baits, topwater lures and crank-baits strung together hook from hook.

But that was all years ago, and I had put it all behind me when I traveled to Kansas a couple of years back to hunt with Jim and one of his buddies on the Fall River, a stretch they knew well. We motored up the stream on opening morning and stopped just before daylight at a spot Jim must have planned on for days.

A gobbler was sounding off only a couple of hundred yards away, and I was grateful to Spencer, my long-time friend and fellow outdoor writer, for giving me the opportunity to hunt such an easy turkey. So I stepped out while he and his buddy motored on to find some other spot. I told myself that apparently old Jim had changed, he was a good friend after all, leaving me with a gobbler which had one foot on a roost and the other one with my tag almost wrapped around it. It was just too good to be true.

And it was a good thirty minutes before I figured out that my old buddy had set me out on an island about two or three acres in size, with a gobbler sounding off on a roost beyond the island in timber I couldn't reach because of a thirty foot channel behind it. And there I sat for three hours, vowing revenge. But in the meantime as luck would have it, I called a gobbler and several hens across the river to my island, and I was the only one who filled a tag that day. And that's part of the reason I haven't thought up some childish prank to get even. I'm beyond that kind of nonsense. Spencer isn't. He's a dirty, rotten, no-good skunk and I'm sorry you folks had to get in the middle of this.

Well I got to thinking about it later anyway, and one day this fellow and I were talking about that Kansas trip and he asked me, "To what do you attribute your success with that gobbler on the Fall River," or something to that effect. And that's when it came to me. I was successful that day because I was trapped on a little-bitty island and couldn't go chasing after that gobbler to botch everything up. I had to sit there and sit there and sit there and wait. Well I gave that a lot of thought and then a week or so later I was down at the local pool hall and some young guy who was trying to get his first gobbler asked me if I had some advice to help him. Did I ever? And I'm willing to tell you just what I told him.

It isn't anything complicated. Just go out and find the best place you can find to hunt, get yourself a big oak you can lean back against and get some cover out in front of you which will hide you from the turkey but won't hide the turkey from you. Now this needs to be a place where the gobblers are roosting not far away, a place you know they are using for early morning mating, or feeding, or passing from one place to another.

When you have that spot, take a pack with some candy bars and sandwiches and a thermos of coffee or a canteen of water, whatever it takes to make you happy. Some folks might would rather have some twinkies or fruit pies than candy bars. Frankly I'm not much on candy bars. I once carried around some extra weight on all my hunting trips due to a great love of donuts and pastries. But I'm getting off the subject here.

Get there on opening day a good fifteen minutes before the gobblers begin to sound off... and take your wife or somebody you can really trust. And I can't emphasize this enough... it must be someone you can trust, because you want them to take a good strong length of chain and a lock and secure you to that tree so you can't leave, and this person who's keeping the key to the lock has to be someone you can depend on to return at noon and unlock you.

Securely situated in a spot where you have to remain, well hidden, your chances of getting a gobbler in range before the noon whistle is extremely good.

The reason most of us fail so often is the problem we have sitting in one place for long periods of time. I myself am constantly thinking of greener pastures on the other end of the ridge, or wondering if I couldn't get a better angle on some gobbler that has stayed out of range longer than 30 minutes. I've hunted so long and goofed up so often that I know I'd be better off to set there and wait, but it's just so hard to do. Truth is, when I was sitting there on that island in Kansas listening to that gobbler across that river, I gave some thought to trying to swim across it. Sitting doesn't seem like hunting. sneaking along and trying to get closer seems more like hunting. And that, my friends, is what ensures the survival of so many gobblers, turkey hunters who just can't sit still and wait.

Now I've never tried this chain and lock idea, but my wife agrees it should work. She says I'd never have to worry, she'd come back and unlock me at noon if she wasn't really busy with something. I think I could depend more on one of my good hunting buddies. Take for instance Robert Murders, who I hunt with often and is pretty reliable for someone who hangs around with people like me. I'd feel better if his name was Robert Smith or Robert Jones but still and all, I think he can be trusted. He's certainly not anything like that dirty, rotten low-down skunk I use to hunt with that left me on that island on the Fall river.

Chapter 14

The Gobbler
Across the Gulch

*T*he two ridges ran parallel to each other, flat on top and not very far apart. They were close enough so that the old gobbler on one could easily hear my timid call from where I stood on the other. The only complication was the boulder-strewn ravine between us, 100 yards across and 2 1/2 miles deep. Or so it seemed.

Some folks say you can't call a gobbler down one hill and back up another. But it can be done. A gobbler in any situation will do what he wants to do and it was obvious he wanted to come over to my ridge. The canyon made him hesitate.

Men and tom turkeys have little in common. There are few men, who, in the same situation as the gobbler, would have hesitated to charge down into that chasm and up the other side if called upon to do so by a fair young maiden. But there is no chivalry

---

Back in the early days, it seemed every gobbler was on the other side of a ravine, or a canyon, or a creek too deep to cross. And in the early days I always went to them.
Seems like they never came to me.

among wild turkey gobblers. That tom expected the hen to cross the perilous gorge and find him.

It was discouraging. I sat calling every 30 seconds and the gobbler just kept answering but never moving closer. It would have been a simple matter for him to fly across to me, but the turkey sat tight. Gobblers are not very intelligent creatures, and he probably never thought of flying over to my side. In time, he might have crossed the ravine on foot, but time was something I didn't have. I was hunting in southern Missouri, it was 11 a.m. and Missouri law requires hunters to clear the woods by noon. Missouri law, however, does not require turkeys to halt all lovemaking by noon, and that's where he had me. He could wait for hours. With that in mind I made my decision. I would move back up my ridge a few hundred yards, then, out of sight and hearing, slide and bounce to the bottom of the gulch. Then I'd climb carefully up the other side to the gobbler's ridge where I would lay strategy for his ultimate trip to the check station.

It was no real problem getting to the bottom of the canyon, I thought as I lay there waiting for the pain to subside. Luckily, nothing was broken so I crawled to my feet and found my gun. It came to me then, a horrible feeling that the gobbler, uneasy over the silence of the hen across the ravine, might have flown across to investigate. When I gained the top of that incline, would I be there alone? It is precisely this unpredictability that makes the wild turkey the greatest challenge to the hunter. It's tough to fool a gobbler but not because of his wisdom. Wild turkeys are among the most unintelligent creatures in the woodland. I've seen them cornered against a fence they could easily fly over, frantically trying to go through it just because they could squeeze their heads through an opening. At daybreak you can hoot like an owl, or slam a car door and a tom will gobble in response, giving himself away. Intelligent? Not the wild turkey. He stays alive because he is a walking example of fear and caution. He is a bundle of nerves, somehow aware that for centuries his kind have been feeding men, bobcats, coyotes and anything else looking for a good meal.

Turkeys have two extraordinary senses they use to cope with the problem. Their sense of sight is remarkable, and hearing just as keen. Tie those two superb defense mechanisms to lightning quickness and you begin to understand why this creature, living just a twig-snap away from panic, is so hard to bring in.

When hunting season rolls around I turn all thoughts to gobblers and I've had enough success chasing them to make me dismiss reports of crappies in swarming hordes spawning in three feet of water. The wild gobblers I have chased cause me to give little thought to the lunker bass looming in the warming waters of a nearby lake,

It's easy to get hooked on turkey hunting because we have a gosh-awful number of gobblers nowadays. When I come back with a big, old ground-raking tom over my shoulder, others look upon me as a fine turkey hunter. What they don't know is that I spooked three bigger ones that morning and walked away from a fourth just 40 or 50 yards away because he had quit gobbling. Much of my success is due to good hunting grounds. With so many gobblers fighting over roosting space, I've had a chance to make all the mistakes at least twice, and learn from them.

When I first started hunting I was afraid to call. I just knew I'd hit a wrong lick and scare all the gobblers into the next county. The experts all tell you how good you have to be with that call — BALONEY! A 15 year old kid with a week of practice can call up a gobbler. It's certainly no great art and a few bad licks won't scare away gobblers. In fact, I've heard hens in the woods that were terrible at calling. No two hens sound the same, in my opinion.

It's also written that he who calls too often will end up turkeyless. I agree that the call can be overused, but there are times when I have called every 10 or 15 seconds and had a gobbler come right in. This can only be learned by experience. You become a good turkey caller when you get over the fear of the call and use it with confidence. Learn to judge the distance or a gobbler and call according to the circumstance. You also learn that sometimes it is best to put down the call and wait.

But the biggest part of turkey hunting isn't the

Calling gobblers back home on the Big Piney watershed, this is The spot where I killed my first one. I think it was about 1971. Right about the time this picture was taken, you could have never convinced me that I could ever do it.

calling. It isn't even a close second. patience, restraint and experience in the ways of the gobbler and his reactions to certain situations are crucial for success. I've heard experts say what a gobbler will and will not do in certain situations but I'm convinced no one can accurately predict his actions. There are no old toms so wise they can't be called. The stories are colorful but untrue. I know that on any given day, the best of hunters fail. It follows, too, that on any given day a beginning hunter may call up an old tom that has refused to move for a week. It just happens that way. No one knows why.

Some claim that yearling toms, or jakes, won't gobble. Experienced hunters know better. I once called up a jake that strutted and gobbled a dozen times or more. I have also watched half-grown wild turkeys, still in a brood, gobble in October. If you can always tell the difference between a jake or a long-bearded old torn by listen ing to the gobble, you have a great set of ears. Sometimes you can, and sometimes you can't.

Time spent in the woods is the best teacher. In 10 years of turkey hunting I have, at one time or another, seen all the old laws broken. "The gobblers won't gobble if it's cold," they say. Several years ago a friend of mine in Arkansas called up and killed a tom that gobbled repeatedly in 30 degree weather, with three inches of snow on the ground.

During the 1975-76, turkey season, we got up one morning to scrape a thick frost off the windshield of the old pickup. It was 29 degrees at dawn, and not much warmer at 10:30 when I killed a 20-pound gobbler sporting a nine-inch beard. He had gobbled as though it were 60 degrees, as did half a dozen others that morning. There are hunters who kill turkeys which gobble in steady rain and those who stalk the woods on beautiful days when all is quiet. Who can explain it?

I first learned to use a call in the early '70s but was terribly afraid I'd use it wrong in the clutch. An experienced hunter who was with me one morning advised patience. They weren't gobbling, but the woods were full of turkeys. I sat down and began to call sparingly. After 20 minutes of silence, I decided to get up and search for a better place I don't know why beginners do such things but when I stood up, heavy wingbeats brought my attention to a pair of turkeys approaching from the rear. The birds were almost in range and they taught me quite a lesson, or so I thought. Later that day I did the same thing. I now realize that toms don't always gobble on their way to a call. If you can't sit patiently for a couple of hours in such a situation, you might as well stay on your feet because it sometimes takes a while for a gobbler to come to you. Some inexperienced hunters think they have lost their turkey just because he quit

*The very first gobbler... an 18 pound jake. He came from a high
ridge overlooking Arthurs Creek In Texas county, Missouri,
April of 1971.*

gobbling. I remember a tom turkey that gobbled for
an hour in answer to my call without coming closer
than 150 yards. Suddenly, he shut up for 20 minutes.
I nearly got up and left, but the experience gained

from the past failures told me to stay put despite the discomfort. When the turkey broke the silence with his final gobble he was only 40 yards away. I never saw him move in through the underbrush.

The formula for success is simple: You learn about gobblers by hunting them, and from the heart-pounding anticipation that often ends in disappointment as you learn.

Some hunters are obsessed with killing a wild gobbler. A few I know boast of a dozen long-range shots each year. Those hunters have no patience or confidence so they attempt to kill turkeys at 70 or 80 yards. They bag a few birds, but most are never recovered. Other hunters sneak in before first light and kill toms off the roost. These people miss everything that makes turkey hunting worthwhile.

I'll keep hunting them as it has been done traditionally. No other way can offer the same excitement and satisfaction. Hunting must be more than just bringing home a turkey. Every trip is an entirely new and different experience and you'll find that gobblers follow no rules. Such was the case on the morning when events brought me to the edge of that canyon.

At daybreak I had heard four or five different gobblers. I sat in on the closest one but noticed 30 minutes later that there wasn't a sound anywhere. Why do gobblers shut up so soon? Events had transpired similarly for several days, so I suppose there was a great deal of mating going on. When hens are on the nest, gobblers are more responsive and hunting is often best. When half a dozen hens run to the nearest gobbler after flying down from the roost, it is somewhat difficult to call that gobbler to you. By 8:00 a.m. I imagine a tom turkey just isn't interested in another hen.

Although many hunters make the mistake of leaving the woods two hours after the gobbling stops, I decided to stay that morning. I sat listening to the silence until 9:30. As the sun grew warmer and the leaves softer, I fell asleep. It was 10:30 when the gobbling from across the deep ravine woke me. I guessed that after the early mating activity the gobblers and hens had separated. As the morning turned to midday the toms were beginning to seek out the hens again. The gobbler across the gorge from me had probably mated with one or more hens after flying off the roost. Then he may have fed for a while as the hens became more interested in adding eggs to the nest. Late in the morning he became lonely and began to gobble in response to my call. After all, a hen with a sorry voice is better than no hen at all.

Twenty or 30 minutes later, I found myself climbing the opposite ridge on all fours, scratched, bruised, scraped and fairly confident I was on a wild turkey chase.

As I topped the ridge about 200 yards from the gobbler, I rose to my weakened knees, blew the dirt out of my gun barrel and reloaded. I reached for the cedar box and gave forth my most seductive call.

The gobbler answered immediately and was exactly where he had been for the past 30 minutes. My knees grew stronger as I headed toward the tom. I moved about 50 yards and called again. The gobbler answered, and the leaves and buds shook. He had moved closer, too. We were less than 75 yards apart, with a thick grove of five-foot pines separating us.

Realizing there was no time to hide, I just sat down inside the thicket of pines. As the gobbler continued to answer. I called once more, very softly, and he really began to sound off. I put down the call, brought my gun up and braced my elbows against my knees to keep the barrel from shaking. The woods grew silent as I peered into the open area where I knew he would appear. suddenly I heard a deep, vibrating, booming sound, so close it seemed as if the strutting tom was right beside me. Instead of moving into the open, he had moved right around the edge of the pine grove. When I spotted him he was in full strut, just 10 yards away.

The turkey strutted slowly past me. His booming seemed to shake the ground. For some reason he never saw me, but I saw that long beard and the big fully-spread tail. The sun caught the feathers perfectly, giving off more color than ever imaginable. I waited until he stopped strutting. As he turned 35 yards away, head erect, wondering where that hen with the strange voice had gone, I steadied the shaking barrel and squeezed the trigger. He was not only the most responsive gobbler I've ever taken but one of the biggest. The tom sported an 11-inch beard and weighed 24 pounds.

Each April season will bring another hunt, different circumstances and most likely different results. That hunt years and years ago was one I will always remember — hearing the gobbler strutting and booming only a few feet away, then watching him move past so close it seemed I could reach out and touch him. It has been 20 years since I have been there but perhaps that old birds descendants on those Ozark ridgetops hold more exciting experiences this spring for other young hunters who need to learn through trial and error, and gain confidence in doing it.

Chapter 15
Nolan Hutcheson

Nolan Hutcheson killed his first wild turkey in the mid 1930s and probably thought he'd never kill another one, because they closed the season in '36 and didn't reopen it until 1960. I interviewed him in 1990 and he was trying to extend a record no other Missouri hunter can ever equal. Hutcheson had filled every spring tag from 1960 through 1990. He told me then that he couldn't remember how many gobblers he had killed. But quite a few stood out in his memory.

"That first gobbler was a 10 or 12 pound jake." Hutcheson said. "I only crippled the bird, but I went back to town, borrowed a friend's bird dog and found him later in the afternoon."

He told me how wild turkeys had became awfully scarce in the 30s and 40s and early 50s, but he remembered seeing a few on the 300 acre farm west of Houston, Missouri, where he was raised. "Dad wouldn't let us hunt those turkeys because he was

afraid they were being hunted too much by neighbors."

"In the early 50s I saw turkeys on land I own, but there weren't many, and they were small. Those wild gobblers were only 15 or 16 pounds as adults."

When the Conservation Commission began stocking wild turkeys they found an ally in Hutcheson. Commission personnel didn't have to stock his land.

"I went to Salina, Kansas in 1956, and purchased seven wild turkey hens and two wild gobblers. These were semi-domesticated wild turkeys. When the hens would lay, I'd take the eggs and put them under chickens.. the turkeys just kept laying. Sometimes I'd get 25 or 30 eggs from one hen. We'd usually raise 50 to 60 poults each year, turn them loose and feed the young birds until fall… then they would gradually begin to chase bugs and roam the woods."

Nolan said that over a seven year period he released about 300 poults and watched them take hold to form growing, thriving wild flocks.

"I think over the years there has been some domestic blood introduced to most of the wild flocks in

---

Nolan Hutcheson, the Texas county resident who loved wild gobblers and loved hunting them. If you hunted turkeys in southern Missouri in the '60s '70s and '80s, you probably have met him or heard about him.

the Ozarks," Hutcheson told me. "One turkey has a deep brown tail and another has a lighter, more beige-looking tail, but I haven't seen any indication that one bird is any wilder than the other."

One thing a sprinkling of domestic blood has surely been responsible for bigger gobblers. For several years Hutcheson had the Missouri state record — 32 pound gobbler taken near the community of Bado, Missouri. His cousin had been hunting on land owned by in-laws and had seen a very big bird there. Nolan and he went back the following day at daylight and heard the turkey gobbling in the same general area.

He gobbled so often, and I could see lights from a dairy barn nearby. I began to wonder if he was a tame turkey!" Hutcheson recalled. "But when we drew closer we found him to be about a half mile past the dairy barn, on land we didn't have permission to hunt. We stopped at the woven wire fence and I called several times. The gobbler, maybe 200 yards away, finally flew toward us from the roost and came in at a run. I shot him only a few moments later. When my cousin picked him up, he said he'd go 27 or 28 pounds. We didn't dream he'd be a record."

Why did the gobbler grow so large? Hutcheson said Conservation Commission biologists examined the digestive tract, and there was only one acorn and some blades of grass in the crop. "The dairy cattle had much to do with his size," Hutcheson theorizes. He had been following them, turning over dried manure, searching out grubs and eating undigested grain.

That turkey had a nine-inch beard and was judged to be 4½ years old. But the real eye-opener is the 13½ inch beard in Hutcheson's collection, longer by an inch and a half than any this writer has seen.

Hutcheson did indeed make an effort to go after big gobblers. He admitted that on occasion, when he had passed up a young jake early in the season, he had often come to wish he hadn't before the season ended.

"One year," Nolan told me with a laugh, "I was convinced my streak was over. I was walking back to my pickup with about 30 minutes left in the season. I actually walked right up on a young gobbler and when he flew I dropped him. I didn't feel bad about killing a jake that year."

I asked Hutcheson if he felt any pressure from his record accomplishment. "None at all," he said, "I wouldn't lose a bit of sleep if I didn't get one this season. I'm out there to enjoy the hunting, and believe me, when I hear a big gobbler drawing close my heart flutters just as much today as it did 30 years ago.

It wasn't exactly 30 years of one success right

after another. Nolan had his share of failure, as have all turkey hunters. One instance he told me about was a real classic.

"A local business was sponsoring a contest several years ago to give an award for the biggest turkey," Hutcheson told me that day in the spring of 1990, "So I was asked to go by the local radio station and make a tape promoting the contest. I spent some time giving some calls and told all I knew about turkey hunting, which didn't take long. The next morning on opening day, I went hunting as usual but I had to get back early and take my wife to Springfield. I was walking up a small cattle trail along a creek bottom when I heard a gobbler sound off high on the ridge. It sounded a long way off, so I leaned my gun against a tree and listened. When he gobbled again, I moved to a flat open space a few feet away, leaving the gun where it was while I had a cup of coffee. I just called once, and a gobbler pitched off the ridge on the wing and sailed right down over me, landing only 20 or 25 yards behind me. I had to make a dive for my gun, but it was too late, the gobbler took off. Shortly afterward, driving home to pick up my wife, I turned on the radio and listened as my own voice told me to always have the gun cradled and ready when waiting for a gobbler."

Years later in the spring of 1997, on a quiet, cool, gray morning, I stood on a lonely ridge listening for gobblers and thinking about that story Nolan had told me. I thought back 25 years to the day I killed my first gobbler, and the man who was largely responsible for that first success.

Nolan owned the land I was hunting that day In fact he owned thousands and thousands of acres and most of it was home to flocks of wild turkeys. A successful businessman in Houston, Missouri, where I went to high school, Nolan was a wealthy and influential man in Texas County and I was just out of college with no money and very little influence. There wasn't a reason in the world for Mr. Hutcheson to give me permission to hunt land that everyone wanted to hunt. But he did. In fact, he took me to the very area where he himself hunted, and told me everything he knew about wild turkeys.

When I called up and killed that first gobbler, Nolan was listening not far away. He came up and shook my hand and congratulated me and seemed just as excited as I was. It was a day I will always remember, and on that opening day of the turkey season in 1997, for some reason I was thinking of Nolan as I stood on that ridge just before dawn. I wondered if he was hunting somewhere over in Texas county, as he had done on opening day for 40 consecutive years. He wasn't.

Nolan passed away on the morning of the opening day of the turkey season in a Springfield hospital at the age of 84. He left this world on a day that was always one of the special days in his life, because Nolan Hutcheson absolutely loved to hunt wild gobblers and he was very good at it.

I hunted his land on Arthur's creek, a tributary to the Big Piney, for about 20 years, driving up each spring from my home in north Arkansas to hunt with my dad and brother-in-law, and always spent some time talking turkeys with Nolan. He told me about 10 years before that he had been diagnosed with a form of. bone cancer, but he didn't intend to let it slow him up any. And I never saw any evidence that it did. He hunted with the energy of someone half his age, and you would have never guessed he was in his mid-seventies then.

He was always tickled to take someone who had never hunted and help them learn to hunt gobblers. Many a beginner bagged their first tom with Nolan doing the calling. He especially loved to take his wife Carolee and she became an accomplished hunter herself. Nolan was never as excited about a turkey he killed as the one's Carolee bagged. He delighted in her successes.

In fact, he delighted in the success of everyone. I never killed a turkey back in those early years without trying to find Nolan first thing and telling him all about it. Every detail from beginning to end — and he was always excited to hear about it.

I didn't learn about his death until after the funeral, but my dad said there were so many people in attendance it would have been difficult to get into the church. Still, I would have liked to have been there. Seems like turkey season in Missouri should have been suspended on that one day, just to honor a veteran turkey hunter and a turkey hunters friend.

But when it comes right down to it, I liked Nolan Hutcheson for a lot of reasons besides the fact he was a fellow outdoorsman. He was a highly intelligent, energetic man who lit up the room he was in with his enthusiasm, and it never dimmed with age. He was generous and hard working and courteous and he put everyone on the same level. You couldn't help but enjoy being around him.

And I know this may sound a little strange to some people but I wonder if, on that final day of his life on earth, as another spring turkey season opened, the Good Lord saw fit to let Nolan return to the turkey woods over on Arthur's Creek in spirit for awhile, to be where he loved to be in the glory of mid-April.

I'm very glad I got to know Nolan Hutcheson, he was a good man, a good friend, a good conservationist and a good turkey hunter. We'll meet again someday I'm sure... and talk turkey hunting once again.

Chapter 16

Make Your Own Call

I finally got into hunting wild turkeys in the early 1970s. It was something new to many Ozark hunters because there were several decades during which the wild turkey had ceased to exist in much of the region's forests.

Old timers like my grandfather had hunted wild turkey 30 or 40 years before, and most of them had made their own turkey calls. By 1970, a new generation of experts were touting an assortment of calls and many of them weren't simple to use.

I tried everything when I was getting started, and began to believe that a wild gobbler couldn't be called within gun range. But all that changed one April morning when I returned from another frustrating hunt and stopped in at a local hardware store. In a cigar box on the counter there were three or four little box calls, obviously hand made. An old man had brought the calls to the store a day or so before, and they were inexpensive, only $2.00 each. I bought one, just to have a new type to go along with all the others

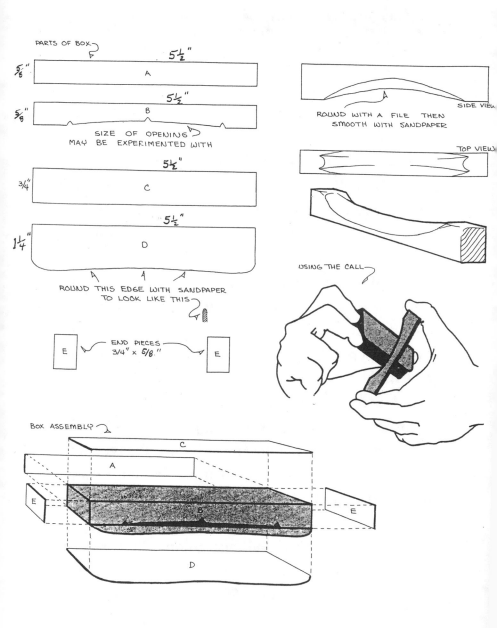

PARTS OF BOX

$5\frac{5}{8}$"

$5\frac{1}{2}$"

A

$5\frac{1}{2}$"

$5\frac{5}{8}$"

B

SIZE OF OPENING
MAY BE EXPERIMENTED WITH

$5\frac{1}{2}$"

3/4"

C

$5\frac{1}{2}$"

$1\frac{1}{4}$"

D

ROUND THIS EDGE WITH SANDPAPER
TO LOOK LIKE THIS

E

END PIECES
3/4" x 5/8."

E

SIDE VIEW

ROUND WITH A FILE THEN
SMOOTH WITH SANDPAPER

TOP VIEW

USING THE CALL

BOX ASSEMBLY

C

A

E

E

D

I had used to no avail. That afternoon I practiced with it, noting that it wasn't very loud, but it sounded more like a hen than anything else I had used.

The next morning, thirty minutes after sunrise, a wild gobbler walked up out of a ravine to within 30 yards of my shaking gun barrel, gobbling as he came. I had used the little call to take my first gobbler, and within a few days, I used it to call up and bag another. To someone who had experienced weeks of frustration, all that seemed like a minor miracle. I rushed back to the hardware store to buy more of the home-made box calls, but they were gone. I tried to find the old man who had made them, but I was a few days too late. The old turkey hunter had died one morning in April while on his final turkey hunt.

There was nothing left to do but try to make my own. Since that day in 1971, I've made hundreds, I suppose, and I've used them to bag more than 70 gobblers, and call up about 50 for other hunters I've guided on spring turkey hunts.

It is true that calling is a small part of turkey hunting, but too often the diaphragm calls used by inexperienced hunters are too loud when a gobbler gets within 100 yards. The box call I use is soft, and beats anything I've ever heard for imitating a hen turkey.

For some, the little box call is just too simple. It really doesn't look proper for a genuine authority to carry around a home-made box call when there are calls available that are twice as difficult to use. If calling contests are your thing, you won't want this call, but as a friend of mine once said, "There are those who call gobblers, and there are those who kill them." I have no time or energy for contests. I'm interested in hunting wild gobblers, and nothing I've ever used has produced the results experienced with this economical little call.

You can make dozens of them in an evening in your workshop. You need strips of western cedar cut out on a table saw. I make most of my calls out of wood strips of two sizes. The strips are about 1/8 of an inch in thickness, the sides are usually only 5/8 to 3/4 of an inch in width, and the top lip 1 1/4 to 1 1/2 inches wide. I make the calls of various lengths, and I've found that size can vary. Experiment with different sizes to see which one you like best. The hardest part is cutting those thin strips, about 1/8 inch thick or a little thinner.

The call is easily put together with a hot glue gun. Shaving down the lip of the call causes the sound to become higher. Your call will be too coarse and deep when you finish it, and must be tuned by taking small strips off the lip.

The striker must be chalked liberally--any type

of chalk will work. Hold the solid striker between the thumb and middle finger of the left hand. Hold the box loosely in the right hand, by one end. The lip of the box should be at the top and scraped downward on the striker at a slight angle.

In one evening, I'll make 20 or 30 calls, and usually half of them are only so-so. Usually though, there will be six to ten in the batch that are excellent. Since they are fragile, you'll need several.

Experiment with the sizes and you'll find there's plenty of room for variation. No two will sound the same, and *none will be as loud as the other calls you've used.* That's the key, though few hunters believe it.

I use these calls in spring and fall. They will produce yelps, cackles, clucks, whines, purrs and putts — all the sounds a turkey hunter likes to play with, even when he doesn't need to.

Of course, you have to know what a turkey hen sounds like and you have to learn to use the call — a chore that may take 30 minutes of practice. Probably a half-dozen times I've given one of these calls to a hunter who had been using a diaphragm mouth call with no luck, and that hunter used it to kill his first gobbler. You can obtain a softness with this call, and a tone that nothing else can duplicate.

There is a special reward to bringing a gobbler into range with a call you've made with your own hands. It's hunting the way our ancestors did, as this type of call was made and used decades ago by a different generation of hunters.

I wish that I could have met that old turkey hunter from Licking, MO, who made that first call. I never even learned his name. But sometimes on a clear, quiet spring morning in the Ozarks when there's a gobbler out in front of me and the rest of the world seems a million miles away, I feel like I know him pretty well. And I haven't bought a turkey call in years and years.

The little hand-made box calls work like nothing I've ever used. My uncle Norton sat on his and still bagged this gobbler on opening day of 1998.

Chapter 17

The Poker Game

*T*here were four of us around the card table in the tent, listening to the rain drumming down on the canvas. While Norm shuffled the cards Jim thumbed through a book on turkey hunting. What's it say about turkey hunting in the rain?" Dave asked him.

Jim turned a few pages and stopped. "When turkey hunting in the rain," he read, "never draw to an inside straight."

It was the second week of April back in the spring of 1981, and we were camped deep in the mountains of western Arkansas unaware that a series of tragic tornadoes were ripping through the mid-south. All we knew at the time was that it was raining too hard to leave the tent, and we were glad to be camped on high ground. I had set up the card table to hold a pan which was there to catch the leak in the roof of the tent. My friend Dave Meisner, a magazine publisher, hauled out a deck of cards and insti-gated a penny-ante game of poker with a two cent

limit. Something of a compulsive gambler in my college days, I hadn't been in a good game of poker since the winter of '69, when I lost better than 2 dollars in an overnight dormitory game of five-card-draw. I know it doesn't sound like much, but you have to understand I wasn't there on a scholarship. So it was with trembling hands I picked up the cards that Norm dealt, somewhat like a reformed alcoholic might treat a filled shot glass. The roar of rain on the roof was broken only by the rhythmic plink of dripping water hitting the bottom of the pan.

Jim Spencer, an outdoor writer of some repute, sat across from me stoicly examining his cards, his poker face even tougher to decipher beneath the heavy layer of green and black camouflage face paint

It had been a rough outing for me — my elbow throbbed from using it as a brake sliding down a mountain. I had a touch of ptomaine poisoning from eating under-cooked hamburger and a fever blister from lying about how many gobblers I had killed in years past.

Things would get worse... Norm dealt me two pair and gave Meisner three aces. I lost my whole nine cents on the first hand. Spencer loaned me a quarter and dealt another hand. There it was, just after a heavy peal of thunder, a six of clubs, seven of hearts, nine of spades, 10 of hearts and a Queen of clubs. If I could only draw an eight. Sweat poured off my stinging elbow as I decided to go for it. I discarded the Queen... and Dave gave me another. Spencer was right — when turkey hunting in the rain, never draw to an inside straight.

When it was my turn to deal, I had only 16 cents left of Spencer's quarter. Meisner had the rest of it; the richest guy in camp and getting richer.

I added both jokers to the deck to count as aces or wild in straights or flushes. Spencer began to sing "Maverick Didn't come Here to Lose."

With two jacks, I opened for two cents... the limit we set at the beginning. I drew two more jacks. Spencer raised, and I raised, and he raised and so forth until my last 16 cents lay at the center of the table, right next to the water pan. The leak had remained steady, changing from the occasional plink of random drops in a metal pan to the regular plunk-plunk-plunk of water hitting water. The tension was high in the tent — a tentful of tension, you might say. Meisner gave forth a low whistle as I laid four jacks on the table, but Spencer's white teeth shined through his black and green countenance as he tabled three aces. .and those two jokers I had added to the deck.

The rain let up a bit, and Meisner loaned me

another quarter. By the time I borrowed a third quarter from Norm Beattie the rain had nearly stopped, the water pan was nearly full, the cards were cold and my fever blister was hurting so bad I actually felt like confessing in regard to my previously stated turkey total.

Three hands later I was down to four cents again. That's when it happened. Norm Beattie dealt me four hearts; a jack, queen, king and ace... and a joker. I sat there staring at the only royal flush I've ever seen. Spencer opened and my four cents was in the pot. About that moment the sun broke out of the clouds and Meisner thought he heard a distant gobbler. He and Beattie folded, and Spencer suggested we forego the limit to close out with a big pot. I laid my cards face down on the table and began fumbling for my billfold, hoping I still had that emergency dollar stuck in a dark corner. When I found it, Beattie sat stacking the rejected cards, with my royal flush somewhere in the deck. Spencer threw in his hand then took my last four cents and the three of them headed for that distant gobbler, leaving behind them a grown man pleading for just one more hand, tears streaking my carefully applied camouflaged face paint. In less than an hour, it was pouring again, and Spencer had missed the gobbler at 10 steps.

I lay awake that night thinking about revenge — a cedar box call filled with Vaseline, or perhaps peanut butter in the toe of a hunting boot. Nothing seemed appropriate for the crime. But the following morning my big chance came. Norm was with me, the guy who had folded my big hand, trying to learn the finer points of calling. We had spent the first two hours listening to nothing but the wind, but about 8 a.m. we were walking along a ridge where turkeys had been scratching heavily for acorns.

I called twice and a gobbler answered just below the ridge. We dived for cover and I called again. The tom answered again just out of view, coming fast. When he came into sight, he was only 25 yards away. Norm raised his gun slowly and flipped the safety off. As he reached for the trigger, I squeezed off a shot ahead of him, and Norm's first gobbler was mine.

We hurried forth to examine the gobbler with Norm shaking his head and moaning his disapproval.

"I was just about to shoot," he said. "Why would a guy with 47 gobblers to his credit rob a poor rookie of his big chance... I had 'im I tell ya...I had 'im."

As I wrapped my tag around the gobbler's leg I smiled for the first time in two days.

"Yeah, Norm, you had him," I said defiantly, "but I had a royal flush."

Chapter 18

A Little Luck Goes a Long Way

Missouri finally adopted a three-week season for turkey hunters in the spring of 1998, after a considerable amount of argument and debate. Arkansas once had a five-week season which has been scaled back a few days. But a hunter who hunts in both states has plenty of opportunities to bag a gobbler. It looks as if it would have been easier than it was that spring.

I had hunted several days in both states without aiming my shotgun. I took another hunter who bagged one and, toward the end of Missouri's first week, I decided I had to get serious about catching up with everyone else. So I zeroed in on a big gobbler which had been ignoring me fairly effectively. That morning, with all his hen friends abandoning him, he came strutting out of the woods and into a little green field about 200 yards from where I waited in a fringe of timber on the other side. In about 30 minutes he had eased himself to a distance of about 75 yards. In another 10 minutes he would have been on the way to the local check station, had not two dogs from a neighboring farm trailed me to my hiding place and put on a big show of affection for me in plain sight of the gobbler. The gobbler left first, then the dogs, with me behind them hurling rocks and insults in their general direction. For the next three mornings I worked on that old gobbler, and watched him come out of the woods and strut around on the other side of the field. He would look my way and fan his tail and snicker to himself and thank the Good Lord for those neighbor dogs.

I am not the kind of hunter to shoot a gobbler off the roost, or ambush one. I won't even use a decoy. My code of ethics refrains me from anything but the pure basics...If I don't call him within range strutting and gobbling, he goes free. But after a week of that, my code of ethics had become strained and tattered and my patience worn plum out. On day number eight, I knocked that alarm clock off the headboard at 5 a.m., staggered red-eyed and haggard toward the coffee pot, donned mud-spattered camouflage clothes and declared war on that gobbler. Ethics be danged!

As dawn crept across the timbered hills, I was sitting there in a brush pile where that old gobbler always came out of the timber. He would think I was on the other side of the field where I had always been, and I would leave my call in my pocket and clobber him from ambush. I would never be able to look myself in the mirror again, but I would eat wild turkey for supper... a once-proud sportsman reduced to a shameless meat hunter.

There were actually two brush-piles — small ones. One lay before me, and one at my back, sort of embracing me with a concealing thicket from behind. To my right was the opening where he always appeared and strutted, and I didn't take my eyes off it. Not a gobble did I hear until 7 a.m., when, as you might suspect, a tom sounded off across the field where I had been sitting for the past week. Twice, three times, four times he gobbled. And suddenly there was a commotion on the other side of the brush-pile before me, and my big gobbler took to flight, winging his way across the field to fight with the other tom. How he got behind that brush pile I'll never know, but he was there, and then he was gone. I heard him and the other gobbler begin to fight, and so I hauled out my call and gave a few loud yelps, hoping they might race back to my side of the clearing in lovesick quest of a hen. Fat chance!

And so the morning grew quiet and I just sat there, wondering how somebody as good at hunting turkeys as I am, could be so bad at hunting turkeys. Just for the heck of it, I started practicing on my little home-made call to see if I could hear a flaw in it, and that's when it happened. A loud, clear gobble came from the brush pile behind me. A new gobbler from who-knows-where had heard me and was fooled. Now there was only one problem... he was on the north side of the brush-pile and I was on the south. For 15 minutes I called and he answered, surely no more than 20 feet apart. His gobbles shook the ground around me, and leaves drifted down from the dead branches above as he thundered his passion in answer to my call. Boy, was I hidden? Boy, was he hidden!

Eventually he came strutting around the east side of the brush-pile and gobbled his last gobble. He had an 11-inch beard and weighed 23 pounds, probably not the one I was after, but he'd do. I'm a little ashamed of the fact that I considered ambushing that other gobbler. It just goes to show what pressure and exhaustion can do to a person in this type of job.

The pressure increased by the time the third week came around. I had been spending some time with other hunters, and didn't I have a second bird. It wasn't getting any easier to call in a gobbler. For one thing, the gobbling was diminishing, and the woods were changing drastically. The mushrooms were all but gone, and I had already seen one copperhead. In mid-April, you could see a gobbler at 100 yards, and sometimes farther. By the third week, as the green growth erupted overnight in the deep woodlands, it became likely that a hunter would catch his first glimpse of an approaching gobbler when he was within shotgun range.

And on opening day, the hens in my area were roosting in the trees around the gobblers, flying down at first light to mate with them, and running with the toms well into the morning. By week three, most of the hens were staying on the nest all night, ignoring the toms as they began the serious task of incubating the eggs.

The three-week season caused many hunters to do things differently. During the first two weeks of the season, I had missed several days because I wanted to do some fishing, or get some work done around the house. Most years, I would have never missed a morning, but I was thankful for the chance to rest a little more, and fish a little more as well. I figured the third week would provide better hunting, and far fewer hunters. I was right on both accounts. At mid-week I went back to the woods and heard about six different gobblers.

I seemed to be fairly close to several of them, so I hid well in that same old brush-pile next to the small clearing studded with walnut trees. The green grass was higher, leaves were bursting forth on the trees, and it was warmer. But at least it was a place where I could see a considerable distance and I liked that.

To my north, there was an oak-hickory ridge where one tom had been gobbling on the roost. The gobbler I had killed two weeks before had roosted in the same area and came to that same clearing. I was sitting in almost exactly the same spot.

This time, things were happening much slower, but I knew he was getting closer as the morning progressed, in a rambling back-and-forth course. But it always sounded like one bird, moving around on that ridge, wondering why the hen wouldn't come to him. At 7:30 a.m. I caught my first glimpse of him, moving out of the timber into the opening. He strutted forward about 8 or 10 feet and behind him came a second and a third gobbler.

Over years of turkey hunting, there have been several occasions when I called up two mature gobblers, and occasionally three or four jakes together, but as I think back on it, I don't ever remember calling in three mature ground-rakers together. This would be a first in other ways as well. I tried to evaluate which of the three was the largest tom, but they seemed to be about the same. The beards were all about 11 inches long, each about the same thickness. They seemed to be carbon-copy gobblers, and now when one gobbled, the other two quickly echoed the report. They eased into range as I called one more time, and with heads high, they stood watching for the hen. Then they moved closer, gobbling again in near-perfect unison. A little closer, a little closer, into a sunlit opening where the first rays of the morning caught the brilliant colors of the dark breast feathers.

I centered the gun barrel on the middle gobbler, and let them gobble one more time. When the heads came up high, I pulled the trigger. Instead of the explosion of a twelve gauge magnum load, there was clank of a firing pin hitting a dead shell.

A lot of thoughts go through your mind after something like that. I wondered for a moment if I had forgotten to load the gun, but I knew I had. Then there was the surprise to see the toms hadn't ducked and headed for the timber. They were still there, with heads high. As a quail hunter might do on a covey rise, I quickly ejected the shell and hurried the second shot. This time the woods echoed the blast and the middle gobbler went down immediately. My turkey season was over.

But the spectacle had just begun. Many times I've heard the stories of two gobblers traveling together, and one jumping on his fallen comrade after the blast of a hunters gun. I knew it happened, but I had never seen it...until then. As my tom went down, and began to flop around as most turkeys do for a few seconds after they have died, the other two began to fight with him, and each other. For almost a full minute they jumped on the fallen tom and spurred him and flogged him without sympathy. When I stood up, they ran off about 40 yards and stood there watching. When I called again, just imitating a hen with my mouth rather than my box call, both birds gobbled in reply. They ambled off as I walked out and tagged the gobbler I had shot. He had one-and-a-quarter-inch spurs, and an 11-inch beard, likely a four-year-old tom. But he weighed less than 20 pounds. I figured that I had indeed been pretty lucky... despite the dogs and the misfired shot-shell, the longer season had allowed me to hunt more, and experience success I might not have had a year before in the same circumstances.

So, in the lush green growth of mid-May, it was all over. Summer was upon us and Spring was gone. The days of redbuds and dogwoods and gobblers and morel mushrooms are too quickly gone. But never forgotten!

For more information about other books written by Larry Dablemont please write to:

Lightnin' Ridge Books
P.O. Box 22
Bolivar, MO 65613